A Child
Like That

FELDHEIM PUBLISHERS Jerusalem / New York

A Child Like That

RIVKA
WALBURG

The names of people and places in this book have been changed, except for the following:

Rabbi Dr. A. H. Fried, who deserves recognition for his devotion and tireless efforts in establishing special education programs for Jewish children; Rabbi Moshe Feinstein z"l, Rabbi Yaakov Ruderman z"l, and Rabbi Yaakov Kaminetsky z"l, three of the renowned *gedolim* of this century; Rabbi Yaakov Weinberg, a contemporary great rabbi, and presently *Rosh Yeshivah* of Ner Israel in Baltimore, Maryland; PTACH and Limudei Hashem (now called Magen Avraham), two Jewish special education facilities, each with its own individual approach but united in their dedication to providing much-needed help and support for children with learning disabilities.

Library of Congress Cataloging-in-Publication Data

Walburg, Rivka
    A child like that / by Rivka Walburg
      p. cm.
    ISBN 0-87306-595-6 (hc).
      1. Learning disabled children—Education—Canada—Case studies.
2. Learning disabled children—Education—Israel—Case studies.
3. Special education—Canada—Case studies. 4. Special education—
Israel—Case studies. 5. Education—Canada—Parent participation—
case studies. 6. Education—Israel—Parent participation
—Case studies   I. Title.
LC4706.C2W35 1992
371.97924—dc20   91-44961

First published 1992

FELDHEIM PUBLISHERS
POB 35002 / Jerusalem, Israel

200 Airport Executive Park
Spring Valley, NY 10977

Printed in Israel

Dedicated to all the wonderful
members of my family — and to the
caring teachers, professionals, and
parents of children with handicaps,
who devote much love and attention
in order to help each child reach
his/her potential.

להקב'ה אני פונה
בהודיה ותפילה
שימשיך לתת לי ולכל הורה
את הכוח להמשיך לטפל
בכל ילדינו

Introduction

EVERYONE IS FACED with challenges in life. Things can happen to us or to those close to us over which we have no control. We are all forced to face disappointments and must eventually try to come to terms with them and deal with our plight.

I have found that what works for me is action: *doing* something to try and change things. For me, the healthiest approach has been to *not* give in to my emotions, but rather to become involved in actively effecting a change which will help the problem. If I am not able to change anything, then I work on myself to accept the situation as unchangeable: that's the way it is. But I will become busy in a different activity; I will seek gratification in working on some project or helping someone else. I don't philosophize to myself. I try to act, and through action I am able to cope.

This book is the story of how I have coped with my son Shimmy and his problems. I hope that my story will encourage other parents, and provide insight for educators and other professionals into the needs of children with disabilities — and their parents.

Preface

IT IS FIVE WEEKS before my son's Bar Mitzvah. For observant Jews, this occasion marks a significant milestone in a boy's life. Upon completing his first 13 years, a Jewish boy becomes responsible for his observance of the Written Law in the Torah and the laws called *Torah she-b'al peh* — the Oral Law. His father will make the blessing *Baruch she-petarani...* — "Blessed is the Lord who has absolved me from the responsibility of my son's actions." This blessing is made when the Bar Mitzvah boy is "called up" to make the blessing on the Torah. The calling up symbolizes the boy's becoming a man.

Is Shimmy ready to accept this awesome responsibility? I wonder. Mothers and fathers always worry about this sudden thrusting of their child into the grown-up world of responsibility. Suddenly, their son can be counted in a *minyan*, the quorum of at least ten men required for communal prayers. Now he is obligated by Jewish law to fulfill the commandments he has been learning, and even doing, since childhood.

When Yosef, our older son, became a Bar Mitzvah, only two-and-a-half years ago, I remember feeling such pride. Yosef had learned by heart his entire *parashah*, the weekly Torah portion, to chant on the Sabbath of his being called up to the Torah. He had prepared two intricate Talmudic dissertations that he delivered with an aplomb that belied his 13 years.

But Shimmy — well, he's a different story. Shimmy has a handicap. I use that word because there is no other definite diagnosis that can apply. Many labels have been affixed to him. One after another, they have been discarded as the diagnosis was proven false.

As he approaches the age of thirteen, Shimmy can speak two languages fluently, Hebrew and English; he also knows a smattering of Yiddish. Behind his ears are two long brown *peyos*. Although my husband Yehoshua and I are not chassidim, we let Shimmy "do his own thing" and wear long sidelocks in the chassidic tradition. For over a year, Shimmy has been attracted to the chassidic synagogue in Kiryat Ganim, where we live. He enjoys their melodies, and the warm and friendly atmosphere of their Sabbath celebration.

He has attended various synagogues since we moved to Israel three years ago. At one time he enjoyed the Sabbath afternoon gatherings at the local Sephardic synagogue: he would recite psalms with the congregants and then have a piece of cake with them. Before that, he was a steady presence in the yeshiva in Kiryat Ganim. Their style is very different from that of the other two synagogues — there he would sit with large tomes of Talmud open in front of him and appear to be learning and referring to the different volumes for clarification of a difficult tract.

Shimmy is very round. He has a cute little nose, thick brown hair, friendly dark eyes, and a big round stomach. He is about four feet, ten inches tall and is quite overweight at 135 pounds. What is Shimmy's handicap? He can be described as a slow learner. When I recall his past — almost 13 years of it — I feel, at times, pain. Sometimes I smile. It has not been easy. Memories crowd my mind.

1

"THERE ARE SEVERAL of you parents with children like Shimon. Why don't you just get together and start your own school," declared Dr. Gillman, an old-time pediatrician in Canada. I had asked Dr. Gillman, who had many Jewish patients, to recommend an educational framework for our son Shimon, who was then a slightly chubby, brown-eyed three-year-old. Shimmy, as we affectionately called him, had a big friendly smile and a hug for everyone who greeted him. Aside from his eyes, which were not always focused straight, he was a very cute-looking little boy. He made many sounds and said a few words, but at age three it was apparent that Shimmy was speech-delayed.

I felt angry at this doctor for putting such a burden on me — and on other parents — by suggesting that we start our own school. How could someone like me possibly start a special program! I was a Hebrew teacher of adolescents; I had no training or knowledge of early childhood education, and certainly not the faintest idea about how to deal with handicapped children. And who were these other parents? I felt that

it was difficult enough that I *had* a child with problems —
surely to expect me to find the solutions was unfair.

But let us go back to Shimon. What was his problem
exactly? Why couldn't he speak? What else was wrong with
him?

Shimmy had been born a little early: during the first week
of the ninth month of pregnancy. I was relieved to have
reached the ninth month altogether, since my previous child
had been premature. Little Chaya had suffered from respiratory distress syndrome — the condition that had killed President Kennedy's third child. We had gone through four endless,
anxious days, not knowing if she would live. This time, I was
grateful that I wouldn't have to endure that experience again.

Shimmy weighed six pounds at birth, and was twenty
inches long. He was quite scrawny looking, and in fact until
the age of two he remained thin. And then, at the time that
most children begin to talk, Shimmy began to use his mouth
for something else instead: constant eating. He suddenly
loved to eat, incessantly.

Yosef is two-and-a-half years older than Shimmy, and from
infancy has been a very quick, alert, bright child. Chaya is
one-and-a-half years older than Shimmy, and although because she was premature it took her a few extra months to
"catch up," by the time she was fifteen months old she was
walking and saying words. She is also a bright child. Shimmy
was a friendly baby and very responsive to music. He walked
at fourteen-and-a-half months and attracted people wherever
he went because he was so friendly and outgoing, always
smiling.

When Shimmy was two-and-a-half, our family of five went
to visit my parents in New York. Although I was waiting eagerly
for Shimmy to start talking, I was not really worried at the
time, since he was communicating very well without speaking,
and seemed to be very sociable. Also, I told myself, each child
develops at his own individual pace. Our trip to New York
shattered my illusions. When I visited friends whose children

were close in age to mine. Shimmy's lack of speech became painfully obvious. He was also physically aggressive with all the children with whom he came in contact.

During the visit, Debby, one of my close friends, approached me. A mutual friend, a speech therapist, had asked her to talk to me. She was concerned about the possibility that Shimmy had a hearing problem, which would explain why he was not talking yet. Although I always respected her opinion, and knew her to be highly qualified, I remember that my initial reaction was one of annoyance: "Why couldn't the speech therapist have come and told me herself?" Nevertheless, since Shimmy had suffered from many ear infections, and I knew that this could cause hearing loss — partial, temporary, or even long-lasting — I decided that upon my return to Canada, I would have his hearing checked.

The fact is, I had begun to acknowledge that Shimmy was not like other two-and-a-half-year-olds in other ways as well. Besides not speaking, and being very aggressive, he did not play with toys or puzzles like his siblings had at that age or like the other children did. I had always been determined not to compare my children with one another, but there are certain activities that are considered normal for children. I was becoming concerned.

Shortly after our return to Canada, before I dealt with a possible hearing problem, I took Shimmy to an appointment I had made earlier with a pediatric ophthalmologist in Children's Hospital. (We'll deal with this first, I told myself. Shimmy had been diagnosed, at the age of two, as having strabismus, a condition in which the two eyes do not focus together, causing a double image. To compensate, sometimes a person will shut one eye, or use only one eye, to block out the double image.) From his birth, I had noticed that Shimmy's eyes were not straight, but the doctors I had consulted felt it was just an illusion created by the shape of his eyes and the wide bridge of his nose. I did not agree, and had finally called a pediatric ophthalmologist.

At the visit, Shimmy acted up terribly. He simply refused to sit still; he cried and screamed and squirmed. The doctor wanted to take measurements over the course of several months to see if the condition was progressing or if it had stabilized.

The doctor ran out of patience very quickly. "What is the matter with this child? Why can't he talk? Doesn't he understand? His behavior is impossible — you ought to have him tested!"

I was upset by the doctor's outburst. Surely pediatric ophthalmologists should have a more understanding attitude and more patience with children! I wondered if it was so unusual for a two-and-a-half-year-old to be frightened and uncooperative in a strange and unfamiliar hospital examining room. And what did he mean by "tested"? For what?

Although I definitely did not like this doctor, I decided that I should nevertheless make an appointment with my pediatrician and ask him if he felt that Shimmy should be tested for a hearing problem.

Despite his brusque manner, Dr. Gillman, the pediatrician, was generally very thorough. He expressed concern when I told him that both a speech therapist and the eye doctor had noted Shimmy's speech delay.

"Do you think I should have his hearing tested?" I asked Dr. Gillman.

In reply, the doctor took a tuning fork and tapped it behind Shimmy's right ear. Then he tapped the fork behind his left ear. He repeated this process two or three times by each ear. Shimmy was sitting quietly on my lap, completely engrossed in a toy I'd brought along. He totally ignored the doctor.

Giving me a long and serious look, Dr. Gillman then pronounced what was to be the first of many diagnoses of Shimmy's speech delay — "Mrs. Walburg, I am sorry to have to tell you this: I believe your son is 90% deaf!"

"No! I don't believe it!" I cried. "Why do you think so?"

"Shimmy showed no response at all by the left ear. By the right ear he may have heard a little."

"But he was busy playing, he was all involved in what he was doing. That's why he didn't respond," I protested.

Dr. Gillman sighed and tapped the tuning fork, holding it behind my ear. I heard the penetrating, whirring sound of the vibrating fork.

"Do you hear that?" he asked. "It's hard to ignore. Mrs. Walburg, I am going to refer you to Dr. Fox, a pediatric ear, nose and throat specialist. He is a very good doctor." He wrote out a referral to Dr. Fox, gave me his phone number and suggested that I call immediately. Thus began a series of referrals and examinations.

As I left the doctor's office, I experienced a surprising feeling of relief. I had for some time suspected that there *was* some problem with Shimmy. Now my anxiety and vague dread had a focus, an explanation. There was a problem, but it had a name, and not such a frightening one: a hearing problem, an affliction I could understand! However, I did not believe that my son was 90% deaf. Shimmy had a favorite record, *The London Pirchei*, and he used to sing along with parts of it. He would often make me take off another record and put on this one. He would not have been able to discriminate between records and songs the way he did if he had that degree of handicap. I thought that it was quite likely that he had a hearing loss, but surely not such a severe one.

I remember talking to my friend Deenie on the telephone later that night, and saying, "You know, I am almost glad he told me that Shimmy's partially deaf — I was afraid he might say something worse."

I did not say what I considered worse.

The ear, nose and throat specialist examined Shimmy and found no physical infirmity. He sent him for a hearing test with an audiologist. Over the years I have taken several children for hearing tests, and I have always found audiologists to be very patient and eager to work with children — no matter how difficult the child's behavior may be. The small sound-proof room can be forbidding and frightening, but when cheerful toys and puppets are found there, it becomes a more friendly place for the child. During the test, Shimmy was immediately praised for positive behavior. Although a thorough battery of tests could not be given to him since he would not sit still long enough, the audiologists were able to determine that he did not have a major hearing loss.

Dr. Fox, whom I consulted afterwards, summed it up. "His speech delay is not caused by a significant hearing loss, Mrs. Walburg. His many ear infections may have caused a mild hearing loss that most likely will disappear with time. But he definitely hears well enough to learn to speak. I will refer you to Dr. Evans, a neurologist on the staff at Children's Hospital. He is very good."

2

TWO WEEKS LATER, with the help of Dr. Gillman, I had an appointment with Dr. Evans. As I observed the doctor giving Shimmy a thorough examination, I frankly was not able to see what was unique about this checkup. What was the neurologist doing that the pediatrician had not done? When Shimmy was older, different neurologists asked him to do things with his fingers, such as touching his right thumb to each finger of his right hand. However, from an uncooperative two-and-a-half-year-old, Dr. Evans made few requests.

At this time I already knew that I was pregnant. I was very happy to be expecting another child, especially since I'd had a miscarriage a year earlier and I had suffered a sense of loss for many months afterwards.

Thus my first questions to Dr. Evans were not only about Shimmy. "Do you think that I have to worry about my future children? Is there any indication that Shimmy's problem is an inherited condition? I am expecting a baby — is there anything that I should do or look out for? Do you know why Shimmy does not speak?"

Dr. Evans had few answers for me. "I do not see any reason for you to worry about your future child. I cannot discern any medical problem, and there is no indication of a hereditary or genetic factor. However, you should prepare yourself for the likely possibility that when Shimmy goes to school, he will have learning disabilities."

"What are learning disabilities?" I asked.

Dr. Evans gave me a vague definition. He said that, basically, Shimmy's speech would improve but that he would continue to need some help. I did not understand until several years later, when Shimmy was actually in school, what that meant!

He did recommend that Shimmy have an EEG to rule out any neurological disorder such as a brain tumor or epilepsy. He did not really feel that anything irregular would show up, but this was the usual course to follow for a child who shows developmental delay. After the test we were to return. It was also possible, he added, that Shimmy would suddenly have a developmental growth spurt and catch up to where he should be. Since Dr. Evans did not seem unduly concerned, neither was I. He did, however, make a concrete suggestion: "Take Shimmy to an occupational therapist."

"What is an occupational therapist?" I asked. It sounded so strange to me. "Doesn't it have something to do with vocational training? Isn't he a bit young for that?"

The doctor smiled and explained. "An occupational therapist works on improving fine motor skills." I did not understand the connection between a speech delay and motor skills. No one explained it to me, and I didn't ask.

The occupational therapist, or OT, as they are commonly called, asked me many questions about Shimmy's motor development: his walking, running and climbing. As we spoke, I looked around the room full of colorful and attractive toys. Shimmy occupied himself by pulling various things off the shelves while the OT spoke to me. Later, when she gave him a puzzle with three shapes — circle, triangle and square — he succeeded in doing it right after a couple of attempts. But because Shimmy was not cooperative for long, I don't remember many other details of that first visit. I do, however, remember wondering if I could or should help him with the puzzle. Was it cheating to encourage him?

As a result of this first appointment, the OT determined that Shimmy was below age level in his ability to perform those activities that require the precise movements of the hands and fingers, such as drawing, writing, buttoning, etc. For half an hour a day, I was to implement a program of various play activities that the OT hoped would improve his fine motor skills.

I honestly wondered how I would find the time. To explain that, let me digress a little and describe the pace of our lives in those days. Both Yehoshua and I were teaching at this time in a Jewish parochial school in a large Canadian city. My husband is an ordained Rabbi; he is also a highly qualified and gifted educator, and holds a Master's Degree in Education and Administration. When we got married we went to Israel, and planned to stay; indeed, our first two children were born there.

We left Israel because of financial difficulties, and returned to North America with the hope of working and earning enough money to pay back the $10,000 loan we had taken in order to buy our apartment in Jerusalem.

We lived in San Francisco for one year. My husband's success as a Rebbe (Hebrew teacher) in the Jewish elementary school there earned him a good reputation. Consequently, the principal of Torah Academy, an educational institution in Canada, offered Yehoshua a position in the high school. Teaching older children would give him a better opportunity to make use of his talents, and he happily accepted the job. When Rabbi Shore, the principal, found out that I, too, was a qualified Hebrew teacher, he was pleased with the opportunity to "import" a teaching couple.

To meet the demands of my job, I had to be in school about twenty-two hours a week; Yehoshua was in school for thirty-six hours. Including the many hours of preparation we put in at home, we worked long days. In addition, our home has always been open to guests, and every Shabbos we would invite students for the Sabbath meals. My children basked in the fuss made over them by these teenaged guests at our Sabbath table. And, although I let myself buy some prepared food, for the most part I cooked and baked myself for our *Shabbos seudahs* — our festive Sabbath meals.

Our life pretty much revolved around the Torah Academy community and not our immediate neighborhood, which was all French Canadian. Yosef and Chaya made friends with their classmates, and I would drive them often to visit these friends, the children of our first friends there. With these friends we formed a car pool, and during the long, cold Canadian winter months, when play outdoors was limited, we and our children spent many afternoons together, often visiting the library, or going shopping.

From May through October, when the warm weather came, I would take the children four houses down to a little playground on the street, where there were swings and a sandbox. We spent most afternoons there, after I came home from work. Usually by the end of October it would start snowing and snow would remain on the ground through April.

This was the pace of our lives then, and I was still determined nevertheless to work with Shimmy every day. The OT also had given me guidance in how to deal with Shimmy's fighting (and I had plenty of opportunity to implement her advice in our house full of very young children).

"Hitting him when he hits others is counterproductive," she explained. "It just reinforces and legitimizes his own tendency to use physical messages. There is a method called 'time out' which is worth trying. If Shimmy hits someone, you simply remove him from the situation, tell him he needs 'time out' and put him in a room by himself for five minutes."

I was horrified at the suggestion. "You mean lock him up?" I exclaimed. "It sounds very cruel."

"You aren't 'locking him up' — you are simply removing him from other people because he cannot deal appropriately with them at that time. If you put him alone in a room with no toys, he will not like it. He will not want to stay there. He will want to behave properly so that he doesn't have to stay there anymore. If you are consistent and put him in 'time out' every time he is aggressive," she assured me, "he will soon learn that fighting does not pay. He will want to avoid 'time out.' It will work if you are consistent."

As simple as it sounds, Yehoshua and I had a hard time applying the "time out" method. I was not sure I could bring myself to "lock up" my son, no matter what the OT said. It still sounded like that to me. We finally did lock Shimmy in the bedroom one day, after he banged Chaya on the head with a wooden block. My sympathy and compassion was all for little Chaya, who, it seemed, always bore the marks of Shimmy's frustration. First I put ice on Chaya's head, and then I took Shimmy to the bedroom.

"You are going for 'time out'," I told him firmly. "You are not allowed to hit. In five minutes you can come out." I locked the door.

Shimmy began to cry piteously. He was frightened. He knew he had done something wrong. I let him out after three minutes. It was all I could take — and anyway, I figured, he does not know the difference between three and five minutes. Every additional minute of his crying was just agony for me.

When I opened the door I comforted Shimmy. He was very upset.

Less than an hour later I heard Chaya's wail. He had hit her again.

This time I put him in the bedroom, closed the door and kept it closed for four whole minutes. I did not comfort him as much when he came out crying. Nonetheless, "time out" remained a hard technique for me to use. When people hear about it they often react as I did, for it sounds harsh. But I did learn that it is a most effective method of altering aggressive behavior. It is a lot kinder toward the child to teach him how to behave properly with other children than to let him continue to be aggressive. A child who cannot get along with other children will not be happy. Social skills should be learned at the earliest age possible.

Yehoshua and I were not always consistent, but we tried, and Shimmy did begin to fight less.

Following the suggested program for improving Shimmy's fine motor skills was much more difficult. To begin with, I had to go to four different stores until I found the large beads and shoelaces the OT had prescribed. I could not find any puzzles with squares, circles and triangles in them and finally settled for a puzzle with four different shaped fruits and vegetables. Getting him to actually sit down was an effort. Finally when I tried to get him to string the beads, he was totally uninterested, not even wanting to look at them. I was discouraged. Chaya however joined us right away and played eagerly with them. And Yosef, curious, happily stuck a pin in the new punching bag right after I'd blown it up — before Shimmy even got a chance to throw a punch.

When I went back to the OT, I told her that working with Shimmy for half an hour was simply impossible. He would hardly agree to sit down with me for five minutes. She said I should try twenty minutes then, or even fifteen. "It is very important," she stressed.

Since Canada has socialized medicine, the doctors' visits did not cost me money, but I soon realized that there were many other expenses being incurred, such as carfare to and from appointments, babysitters, and the special new toys I had to find. For blocks, I did not have the cubes the OT wanted, only a colorful multi-shaped set — so I went out and bought cubes.

The idea was to get Shimmy to pile them one on top of the

other. He could do two, and then got to three and even four. I did not understand why that skill had to be improved, but I was embarrassed to report back to the OT that I hadn't accomplished anything.

At her suggestion, I bought construction paper and covered three milk cartons with red, blue and yellow paper. Then I cut out four matching strips of paper in each color. Shimmy grasped this task relatively quickly and would put the red strip of paper in the red box, the blue in the blue box, etc. I increased the number of colors and added various shapes. Shimmy was able to differentiate colors easily, but when I tried to teach him to say the names of the colors, this task proved difficult for him.

Upon the OT's advice, I got Shimmy to sit with me by promising to play his favorite record afterwards — thus he was rewarded for his efforts. Although I found the constant struggle difficult and frustrating, I had to continue. My husband couldn't do it, since by the time he got home, Shimmy would be too tired to concentrate on a task. The OT berated me for not making a greater effort. I often felt guilty.

In the spring I had an appointment for Shimmy with a speech therapist, a Mrs. Sands, for a speech evaluation. Two hours later he was to have his EEG. Dr. Gillman had highly recommended the speech therapist and through his intervention she fit us into her busy schedule. This was the first time in the course of all our running around that I had taken a day off from work. Until then, I had arranged all our doctors' appointments for afternoon hours, or I had switched my classes around.

I took a big bag full of disposable diapers, toys, fruit, sandwiches and Shimmy's bottle. We had to wait twenty minutes to see the therapist and Shimmy was becoming bored and fidgety. I'd brought along a little toy train engine that I would wind up and place on the floor — this toy was useful in getting Shimmy to walk with me down the long corridors of the hospital. But the ploy only worked sometimes; often Shimmy would balk and run away. I also came equipped with colorful popbeads, bought at the recommendation of the OT. He played with these for a short while, but then got tired and wanted to take his bottle and go to sleep.

At that very moment the therapist called us in. Mrs. Sands began by asking many of the same questions that I had already answered with the pediatrician, as well as the ear, nose and throat doctor, the neurologist and the OT: "When was Shimmy born? Were there problems in delivery? Did he nurse? When did he start sitting, standing, walking? What words does he say? When did he first make sounds? Is he toilet-trained? Can he drink from a cup?"

While I tried to answer her, Shimmy was becoming more and more cranky and irritable. I finally laid him in my arms like a baby and gave him his bottle. This interested the therapist, and I knew exactly what she was thinking.

"Of course he drinks from a cup," I said defensively. "He just still takes his bottle for comfort. Besides, my oldest son Yosef, who is exceptionally bright, drank from a bottle until he was three. He could speak and reason like a little grown-up, but he also was not toilet-trained until he was almost three. My daughter was also trained at three. I do not really push it before then — in fact, I haven't even tried yet with Shimmy. I'm waiting until he turns three and the weather is warmer. It will be easier then."

Mrs. Sands, like other professionals, seemed not to realize that when a child is present, but ignored, he will inevitably become bored. She appeared to be observing Shimmy while speaking to me about him, but the fact is that she was not talking to him, only *about* him. What little boy likes to be ignored! And in addition, he was tired and bored. He wanted to go home. When, ultimately, Mrs. Sands tried to get him to look at pictures and play with her, he had had it! He was totally resistant and uncooperative, and finally he just began to cry.

His eyes ran, along with his nose and his mouth.

"Oh, he drools too?" asked Mrs. Sands.

"No, he does not drool," I snapped. "He is just crying."

She then made her pronouncement on Shimmy: "Drooling is just another symptom characteristic of children with delays. He will keep growing and developing, but he will always be just a little behind. Diapers, bottles, they are typical for *a child like that.*" She told me to come back in six months.

I felt humiliated, disturbed and frightened by her words — *a child like* ... what? — but I did not really have time to think about them. I had to calm Shimmy down and occupy him for an hour until the EEG.

"Let's go down to the cafeteria," I told him. There, I bought a cup of coffee for myself and a soda and candy bar for him. I suppose, in retrospect, chocolate bars were not the best food to accustom an already chubby Shimmy to. But I just wanted to keep him happy.

Outside the cafeteria was a large, enclosed play area filled with toys. Shimmy agreed to go in for a short while, and I sat down to watch him. While sitting there, I noticed a boy in a wheelchair watching the others. He was blond and had a beautiful face. One of his hands seemed to be swollen to unusually large proportions. I remember him particularly because his face was so sweet, but there were other handicapped children there as well who had all kinds of problems. They were all in the hospital for different evaluations and treatments. Shimmy looked so *normal* to me, and I remember wondering if all the other parents were trying to figure out why we were there!

Afterwards we made our way to the room where the EEG was to be done. By this time, he was absolutely exhausted. He had not had his usual morning nap and it was already after 1:30 P.M. Just as he was falling asleep on my lap, the technician finally called us in for the EEG.

Carrying him in, I placed him gently on the examining table. Suddenly he opened his eyes, looked around at the various kinds of strange machinery around the table, and began to scream. One nurse tried to calm him and held his hands down while another began putting a jelly-like substance on his head — this was for the little tabs with wires attached. Although it was all painless, Shimmy was terrified and very overtired. He simply became hysterical. And I? I felt like crying myself and suddenly was overcome. "I'm going out," I told them in a broken voice that I could not control. "When should I come back?"

They told me that I could come back in about twenty-five minutes. I ran out crying, seeking the privacy of the ladies' room. I could still hear Shimmy screaming as I rushed down the corridor. I could not bear it and ran up a flight of stairs to the bathroom on the next floor. But I could hear Shimmy's screams even there. Desperate, I took the elevator up to the very top floor, found a bathroom, and cried uncontrollably for ten minutes. I splashed cold water onto my face and wiped the smeared mascara. Immediately I felt tears welling up again.

I had not cried at any point before over Shimmy. Not at the beginning, not at any of the evaluations and consultations. I had denied to myself that any real problem existed, insisting that all these tests were just to rule out any doubts I or anyone else might have. Shimmy was perfectly fine! Sometimes after seeing Dr. Long, the eye doctor, I had felt ill at ease because Shimmy was never cooperative and Dr. Long was always annoyed. But I attributed my discomfort to Dr. Long's impatience — not to Shimmy's behavior. Shimmy was the baby of the family, and I adored him. But I knew that it wasn't only his screams which had upset me now. I was also beginning to absorb what Mrs. Sands, the speech therapist, had implied — in fact, had said. There was something wrong with my little boy.

Shimmy was sound asleep when I returned. All they told me was to wash the sticky jelly out of his hair with shampoo when we got home. Technicians do not give results. They added that Dr. Evans would interpret the test for me at our next appointment.

I took a taxi home. Shimmy was happier after having slept a little. I turned on the television for my kids and climbed into bed, totally drained, physically and emotionally.

Three weeks later Dr. Evans informed us that the EEG was normal. "We can rule out petit mal, minor epileptic episodes, as well as other things, as being a cause for his speech delay. Physically Shimmy seems fine. He has some minor delays in his motor skills but I would just wait, and I'll see him again in six months. In the meantime I urge you to continue the exercises and games the OT has recommended." (The OT had given me many helpful suggestions in dealing with Shimmy, besides "time out." She had explained the concept of positive reinforcement — how rewarding a child for his accomplishments is very important. This acknowledgment can be with a toy, a treat, or even a smile and a "thank you." With Shimmy we made an effort to acknowledge all his efforts, even small ones. We learned to say a modest "good try" or "nice job" even when a task was not completed. When he did accomplish the desired end he was lavishly praised.)

At that time I was still prepared to try, but in retrospect I think that the recommendations of Dr. Evans and the OT were not realistic. I was a working mother of three small children, and expecting a fourth. For six months my work with Shimmy had met constant failure. Today I know that my experience was natural, that it is often difficult for a parent to work with his own child, and that an outsider can sometimes achieve more. It depends on the parent and the child — and the situation can even change with one's own child. Six years later Shimmy and I were able to sit together for fifteen minutes at a time. But in those early days I had to adjust to the new situation and had many burdens. I did not find the OT sympathetic; she made me feel that I just was not trying hard enough. Today I wonder why she herself did not give him weekly therapy sessions.

3

WE WERE GOING AWAY for the summer, to a bungalow colony in the Catskill Mountains in New York State. Yehoshua was going to be a a teacher in the mornings and in return we would receive a free bungalow. The children would be able to go to day camp for free. We considered ourselves very fortunate for this opportunity, especially since the OT had suggested sending Shimmy to day camp. She felt that being in a group of other children would provide him with a good opportunity to improve his speech.

Although Shimmy was not fully toilet-trained, I hoped that during the summer he would learn to be. I wanted him to be ready to go into Torah Academy's nursery school in the fall. The head counselor was reluctant to accept Shimmy in the nursery group at camp, for he was still physically aggressive to other children, and he was still in diapers. I tried to assure her that he was already beginning to use the toilet, and that I would send him to camp only after he had had a bowel movement in the mornings. Moreover, I added, he would wear paper diapers as extra protection. And if he were to soil them,

I would come and change him myself.

"And as for his aggression," I explained with more assurance than I felt, "you know, it stems not out of desire to hurt anyone else, but rather as a means of communication. He understands whatever you say to him and he can say some words. But because his speech is limited and sometimes unclear, he uses 'physical messages'."

Shimmy was accepted on a trial basis. At the beginning I hovered nearby, anxiously, every day. At first he would not let me leave, but then a kind young junior counselor took a liking to Shimmy, and he to her. He called her Boo — instead of Sue. She thought he was cute and cuddly and every morning would come and pick him up. Sue provided the perfect incentive to get him to go to the bathroom. "Quick, Sue is coming! You have to make before you go to camp!"

Yosef in the meantime agreed to go to camp for only half a day — he liked the learning in the morning but was not too keen on the sports later. Chaya had started out in Yosef's group. When she said she did not like it and asked to be transferred to Shimmy's group, initially I was opposed to the idea. I knew she was much smarter than Shimmy — why should they be together? It was a small day camp and the groups had children of two years' age span grouped together. I naturally thought Chaya should be with the older group. But when she announced that she was not going to camp anymore with Yosef, Yehoshua said, "Why not let her join the younger children? If she enjoys herself, what does it matter?"

I suspected she was simply jealous of Shimmy, but in the end I agreed to send her to his group. She loved it and won the "best all-around camper" award.

Shimmy also won an award at the end of camp — for the child who showed the greatest growth. He had learned to accept the authority of the counselors; he had learned to follow directions. And when it came to songs — no one was more enthusiastic. His art projects were not executed well — but his efforts were apparent. And last, but certainly not least, his vocabulary had increased. We were happy to see that being among other children had such a positive effect on Shimmy.

Most of the people in the bungalow colony knew and liked Shimmy. The men knew him from synagogue, where he would go to pray every day. My husband has always insisted that our children can come to *shul* only if they behave. Though Shimmy could not really pray, he was a good mimic: he would sit with a *siddur* (prayer book) open in front of him, and mumble along in imitation of the men who were quickly reciting the Hebrew words; he would call out a loud *Amen* at the end of the blessings. His ability to imitate was, and is to this day, a strength that helps him integrate into society.

The whole family had a good summer. I swam every day and even set aside time to prepare my lessons for the next school year. Yehoshua enjoyed the change, working with young children again instead of teenagers.

4

WHEN WE RETURNED to the city, my major concern was: Would Shimmy be accepted into Torah Academy nursery school? In addition to everything else, he still was not completely toilet-trained; I decided I would speak directly to the teachers about this problem and try to enlist their help. I colored the facts, slightly.

"Shimmy has only recently become toilet-trained, so for the first few weeks I would like to leave a diaper on him just as a precaution," I said.

The teachers, *Morah* Rena and her assistant *Morah* Rochel, were both young and single. Rochel and I were somewhat friendly because Chaya had been in her class the year before. Since Yehoshua and I were both teachers, they were inclined to bend the rules a little. (I remember discussing the problem with my friend Bonnie; she told me that her daughter, who had just turned three and was going to be in Shimmy's class, was also not a hundred percent toilet-trained. She had decided not to say anything to the teachers yet, she said; since it was still warm weather, Naomi could wear skirts and the teachers might not notice. With Shimmy it would be harder to conceal an accident.) But I didn't want to pressure him now. He had an eye operation scheduled for mid-October, I explained to the teachers; until then I wanted to keep life easy for him. Right after that, I assured them, we would certainly get rid of the diapers.

All of the Jewish holidays that autumn fell in September; there would be few days of school anyway. The teachers agreed to accept Shimmy on a trial basis. His poor speech presented them with a challenge. I had explained that for Shimmy, nursery school was not a luxury but a necessity to help further his speech development.

During his first two days of nursery school I was able to sit there, and help Shimmy feel comfortable and get used to things. He was a little clingy at first, but gradually he moved away from me and joined the other children. On the third day, because I had early classes to teach, I wouldn't be able to go along and was quite anxious about how Shimmy would react. My friend Bonnie promised to stay and see how he was. Later she assured me that Shimmy had run eagerly from the station wagon — with all the other children — straight into class, and had greeted his *Morah* with a big "*Shalom*" and a smile. What relief I felt.

"You know," Bonnie told me, "it would probably be better if you yourself did not drive him to school — ever. Once he is settled in with the other children in a car pool, he is fine."

Of course this was not feasible since car pooling was the practical way, financially, of getting the children to school. And I had to take my turn along with four other mothers.

As the days passed, though, the car pool became more a source of tension than convenience. Shimmy did not always go calmly into the car pools and sometimes I had to carry a screaming child down the stairs and forcefully put him into the car. During the first two weeks, he sometimes fought in the car as well, and usually it was Chaya who bore the brunt of his aggression. I was afraid that the other parents would not want to continue taking Shimmy.

The tension grew, until every morning was miserable. For one thing, I had to make sure Shimmy went to the toilet before nursery. Even if he had a bowel movement in his diaper before the car pool came, I would feel relief, for then I would not have to worry that he would soil his pants in school. I made him sit on the toilet until the car pool arrived or until he would defecate. Once or twice, though, when he did have an accident in school, the teachers were not overly upset and I was grateful for their leniency.

In the third week of September Shimmy had another eye checkup, and Dr. Long at this time confirmed that the present measurements were probably the best he could get and an operation was definitely called for. The date was confirmed for the middle of October.

I now know many of the questions I *should* have asked the doctor then. I may have hesitantly asked if the operation were absolutely necessary, and what we could hope would be the results. But I did not go for a second opinion. I did not read up on strabismus. Perhaps the results would have been the same — but I regret not "going into" the operation with more knowledge. I am also skeptical about whether the doctor truly had accurate measurements. Shimmy was never cooperative at that age, and constantly squirmed when his eyes were being checked.

What I should have asked is the following:

1. What are the chances this operation will help Shimmy achieve binocular vision?

2. Do you feel confident that your measurements are accurate?

3. What are the risks involved in the actual operation?

4. What, if any, are the alternatives?

5. How long will it take for us to know if his eyes are better?

I also regret that Yehoshua and I did not consult with a rabbi then, and ask for his blessing. People had told us that this operation was simple and routine; many stories of cross-eyed children were presented to us by friends — all with successful endings. We were also encouraged to go ahead by a second cousin in Montreal, who is very pretty and had had corrective eye surgery in childhood. Nonetheless, there is much comfort and confidence to be gained in consulting with an esteemed rabbi for major medical decisions. Any operation involves risk. A rabbi's blessing can only help.

I have since learned that the main reason to perform surgery on a child with strabismus is to help him achieve binocular vision, seeing with both eyes at once. There are different approaches to achieving this goal. An ophthalmic surgeon will try to tighten a loose muscle so that it will have elasticity which is equal to the stronger eye. If one eye is clearly stronger, patching the stronger eye to encourage use of the weaker one is another method used. The idea is to not allow the weaker eye to be "lazy" and rely on the stronger one. Optometrists who specialize in visual therapy believe that eye exercises can train the two eyes to work together.

Shimmy didn't have "lazy eye" — he alternated in using his two eyes. He has equal vision in both, but to this day he can use his eyes together only some of the time. Occasionally he squints, closing one eye, and at those times I suspect he is having some double vision.

At the time the operation was scheduled, I was quite ignorant of these things, and I simply felt, "Let's just get it over with." I was in my eighth month of pregnancy and I wanted Shimmy to have the operation before I gave birth.

Yehoshua was very casual about the operation, and said, "If he needs it, let's do it."

The joyful, week-long Festival of Sukkos was upon us right after the serious Days of Awe: Rosh Hashanah and Yom Kippur. Decorating the sukkah is a great pleasure, but very time-consuming. Each of my children brought home a picture or chain made in school. Shimmy's paper chain had only three loops. It was hung up on the wall next to Chaya's and Yosef's contributions. Then there were all the festive holiday meals to prepare. Who had time to worry about Shimmy's upcoming operation?

Right after Sukkos, Shimmy got a bad cold and croup. On the night of October 10th, his croup was so severe that we took him to the emergency room for treatment. In the morning it was much better, but by then I had a new concern: I was in labor. The obstetrician ordered me to go straight to the hospital when I called him.

"But I have a sick little boy at home," I said. "How can I leave him?"

"Mrs. Walburg, you have *another* child's life to consider now," he replied.

I quickly found a babysitter and called my husband at school.

The whole time I was in labor, I worried. First about Shimmy, and then: "If the baby is a boy, and born after sundown, his *bris* will fall on the day of Shimmy's operation!"

It turned out that our son Yona was indeed born long after sundown — and long after midnight. He was born on the next morning, October 12th, five weeks early. But I didn't have to worry about his *bris*, because he was premature and so frail that it was postponed for two weeks. Once again I had to endure the empty feeling of leaving the hospital without a baby, as I had after Chaya's birth. Thank God, Yona had no respiratory problems, but he was small and weak and needed to gain weight. My anxiety was divided between him and Shimmy's upcoming eye operation.

Two days after I came home, we had to be in the hospital with Shimmy by 8:00 A.M. My mother came from New York to give us much-needed help as well as moral support. We dropped Yosef and Chaya off at different friends' houses, where they would eat breakfast and then go to school. Since Shimmy was not allowed to eat before the operation, we wanted to avoid upsetting him. None of us ate at home that morning.

When the moment came, it was upsetting for all of us. Shimmy did not want to wear the hospital gown, and getting him into it was a struggle. When the nurses came to take him to the operating room he began to cry. I was frightened and empathizing with him, and I began to cry too. But I had no time to give in to my tears: I had to hurry to a different hospital, where little Yona was waiting to be fed. I had to nurse him and leave milk for his next feeding.

As I sat nursing him, it was frightening to think of Shimmy undergoing the operation at that very moment. I tried not to think of the worst things that could happen, but it was hard not to. As I sat there with the other mothers of preemies, I felt my tears begin to fall. "I have a little boy who's having an eye operation right now in the Children's Hospital," I explained to a sympathetic mother. "I am so nervous."

She offered the usual comment: "I'm sure everything will be fine."

I took a taxi back to the hospital and by the time I got there Shimmy was already in the recovery room. They let us in to see him: Only one eye had been operated on, and I could see a few drops of blood on the white of the eye. The doctor patched it, and said we could take him home. He would be groggy for a while, and we should bring him back in two days.

Shimmy suffered the effects of the ether for two days, and he slept most of the time. This was a blessing because as soon as we came home from the hospital with Shimmy, we got a message that Yosef was being sent home from school with temperature of 104 degrees. Chaya came down with the flu the next day. As if this weren't excitement enough, I was running back and forth to the hospital to feed little Yona several times a day as well. My mother's being there was a great help. And fortunately, I regained my strength after childbirth very quickly.

Shimmy had to wear an eye patch for the next few weeks. The doctor wanted us to alternate the eyes to be patched. The idea behind this was to give each eye a chance to work independently and thus become stronger. I noticed immediately after the operation that the eye which had been operated on, now turned in! Previously it had turned out. But Dr. Long assured me that slowly it would move toward the center. He explained, "The muscles around the eyes are like rubber. Before the operation, the muscle was stretched outwardly. Therefore I have overextended the elastic muscles in the opposite direction, so that they will eventually snap to the middle."

Over the course of the following weeks and months, the eye did look straighter but it never assumed a 100% center point. He had "overkilled" a bit. Altogether I view that operation as a failure because in no way was Shimmy's vision improved.

The few weeks of patching also caused problems. Shimmy was self-conscious and very sensitive when other children stared at him, and as a result he regressed and resumed the aggressive behavior that had improved so much. Being in a structured class was very positive for Shimmy, but the eye patch disoriented him and in addition to fighting more, he also regressed in regard to toilet training and had several accidents the first week after returning to school. Very likely, having a new baby at home had its effect on Shimmy's behavior as well.

5

ONE DAY, about two months after Shimmy had returned to
nursery school after his operation, he soiled his diaper. It was
at the very end of the day, and it was our misfortune that I
hadn't arrived to pick up Shimmy before a certain mother
walked in to pick up her car pool children. She immediately
detected the smell and demanded from the teachers the name
of the "offending" child. The teachers had not been particularly disturbed about his "accident": it was at the end of the
day, they did not have to clean him up, it had not interrupted
their lessons, and they were sympathetic to this cute, chubby
little boy who had just undergone an operation and had other
problems. For despite those problems, he always lit up the
classroom with his big smile and friendly "*Shalom*" when he
entered the room every morning.

But this mother was outraged that her child should be
classmates with one who was not toilet-trained. She felt it
"lowered the standard" of the class, and she was determined
to see that Shimmy would not remain there.

I do not know, or care to know, all the details of what

transpired. I first learned that there was a problem when Rabbi Brown — the principal of the elementary school, which included the nursery — called to arrange a meeting with me.

Perhaps I subconsciously blocked out his true message. I left his office after our meeting understanding that he felt Shimmy's presence in nursery was a problem. The school's policy was: no diapers in class. A child not fully toilet-trained could not enter nursery.

"After all," he said, "nursery is a luxury. We have a right to limit registration."

"But, Rabbi Brown," I tried to explain, "for Shimmy, nursery school is not a luxury. It is a necessity. I was advised by professionals that being with other children his age is crucial for Shimmy's speech development. Anyway, he is almost totally trained and it was just the operation which temporarily set him back." This was the truth. The diaper I had been putting on him when he went to school was more of a crutch. At home he did not wear diapers and he was using the bathroom.

Rabbi Brown said that he would send a school social worker to observe Shimmy, and added that he had heard that there were other behavior problems as well.

"The teachers have not complained to me. On the contrary, they seem to enjoy him a lot," I said.

Rabbi Brown replied coldly, "The teachers do not report to you. I am their principal."

Throughout all this, I did not realize that what Rabbi Brown was actually telling me was: "I want to expel your child from my school."

He was visibly awkward in dealing with me, for my husband — who was teaching at the time of the meeting — and I were his colleagues. He also knew us socially. We parted with my promising to ask Shimmy's occupational therapist for advice on dealing with "the problem." He told me again that he would send the social worker to observe, and subsequently he would make a decision.

When I called the OT for advice, she was shocked that the school was judging Shimmy, and suggested that a team meeting be called. All the professionals dealing with Shimmy should meet and give a recommendation as to what educational and disciplinary approaches would be most suitable for him. She personally called the neurologist and set up a meeting for the principal, social worker, neurologist and herself.

The OT seemed to be on my side. The team meeting was set to take place two weeks after my meeting with Rabbi Brown. In the interim, the social worker and the OT were to observe Shimmy in class, and to consult with his teachers.

The teachers had by that time been instructed by Rabbi Brown to keep much of their opinions to themselves.

The social worker was a friendly and sympathetic person who openly told me his impressions. "Shimmy is thriving in the class. True, some of his behavior is immature for his age — he lies on the floor a lot and rolls around, something that most three-and-a-half-year-olds do not do. However, I have not seen any really negative behavior — he certainly does not disrupt the class. For Shimmy's sake, I will recommend that he continue where he is this school year." The OT told me that he did not easily play with other children but that he did have one friend, Jonathan. I remembered that Shimmy had mentioned a boy named Jonathan. The OT suspected, she told me, that Jonathan had some problems too. I do not know if he did. At the time I felt that in saying this, the OT was being petty and picking on Shimmy's friend. For whether he had problems or not, I was very happy that Shimmy had this one friend.

During this period, an unusual incident took place. One of the boys in the class, who was known to be rather tough and aggressive, bit Shimmy very hard on the leg. The teacher called me on the phone to prepare me, so that I would not be alarmed when I saw the bite. I was sorry that Shimmy had gotten hurt, but it is not my nature to make an issue of such things. So I kept quiet.

On the morning of the scheduled team meeting, Dr. Evans' wife was injured in a car accident. He ran to be at her side in the hospital, and the meeting was cancelled.

And so, instead of the team consultation, Rabbi Brown asked me to his office once again. I was apprehensive and wanted Yehoshua to come with me, but he was teaching a class he felt he could not miss. He promised to meet me after his class, and together we would go to Rabbi Shore, who was the Dean and whose authority superseded that of Rabbi Brown.

Rabbi Brown came to the point as soon as I was seated. He said, "I am very sorry, Mrs. Walburg, but you are going to have to keep Shimmy at home. It is our policy that children in the nursery school must be toilet-trained."

"But he *is* now," I quickly interrupted him. "I have taken off his diaper completely. Anyway, why can you not wait for the team meeting? You had agreed. Just because there was an accident and it was postponed, why can you not wait until it is rescheduled?"

"I am sorry, but we cannot wait any longer. I do not know when we can reschedule, and anyway, I do not need any doctor's opinion to reach my decision. Shimmy is not like the other children and we cannot accept *a child like that*. He is immature. He is aggressive and he bites."

Once again, I interrupted him. "What are you talking about? Shimmy does not bite. Last week a kid bit *him* very badly. Maybe you should look into that kid. You didn't hear about it because I just happen to not like to make complaints. You have your story mixed up," I angrily informed him.

"I do not know. That is what I was told."

"Excuse me, but I *do* know," I insisted. "Do you want to see the mark on Shimmy's leg? It's still there."

"That is not the issue, anyway," he replied impatiently.

"The other parents feel that Shimmy, who has accidents in his pants, should not be in the nursery school, which is after all a privilege and not a requirement."

Rabbi Brown was quite adamant and suddenly I felt totally defenseless.

"What do you want me to do?" I asked.

"Do not send him to school anymore!"

There was nothing more to be said. I just rose and quickly left, trying to control myself. I felt nauseous. However, I still held on to the tiny scrap of hope that Rabbi Shore would overrule Rabbi Brown. Yehoshua met me in Rabbi Shore's office and I chokingly told him, "Shimmy's been kicked out!"

I can barely remember the meeting with Rabbi Shore. Yehoshua tried to get him to extend the trial period until they could hold the team meeting. Rabbi Shore said it was Rabbi Brown's decision and he had to support him since Rabbi Brown really knew better than he what was going on in the elementary school. Rabbi Shore was more involved in the High School. There seemed again nothing to say.

We went home. I think back and remember that I felt totally empty. My biggest concern was: What will Shimmy think the next morning when I tell him he cannot go to school? How will he feel?

I called the OT with the verdict, and begged her to help me find some place to send Shimmy. At home we put on an act and didn't let on that anything was wrong until the kids went to sleep. Then I went to bed and cried. "What should I tell Shimmy tomorrow? He is going to be so hurt."

The next day was Friday, and I would be teaching for only two hours. Chaya and Yosef left for school. I tried to tell Shimmy matter-of-factly, "I am sorry you cannot go today." I wanted to make it sound as if it were only for that one day for some reason. He cried a little, but Yona's babysitter, who knew what was going on, was able to divert his attention. I left for school feeling leaden.

The two hours were endless and I was utterly miserable. I

kept running to the teachers' room to make calls. There were two other Jewish nursery schools in town. One of them was high-pressured with much emphasis placed on learning, and this obviously was not for Shimmy. The other one had thirty-two children, far too many for the environment with potential for individual attention which I was seeking. The OT recommended another school, a three-day-a-week nursery which was geared for children with problems. It was a special education, diagnostic kindergarten. Even though it was not Jewish, I was considering it for I did not really have any other options. It sounded like a framework which could help Shimmy, and there were only five to six children in a class. I hesitated because it was very expensive, and I was not sure how we could get Shimmy back and forth. Also, what would he do the other two days of the week?

Many of my fellow teachers in the High School detected my anguish. Respecting my privacy, they did not ask the cause of it, but they offered words of friendship and support which I greatly valued. "Whatever is troubling you so, Rivka," one teacher told me, "I hope it will improve."

Shabbos, our day of rest, was not restful emotionally that week. It passed sadly, for I still did not know what Shimmy was going to do. I feared that when Monday, and then Tuesday, and then Wednesday, came along and he began to understand that he'd be staying home, that he would lose all that he had gained. I began to become angry at these principals who so easily, so callously, could dispose of a child. I could not understand how such a thing could happen to *me*. I, who as a teacher had always fought for keeping problem students, had always felt children must remain in the class and be given another chance, both weak students as well as those with behavior problems.

How could my sweet little boy be thrown out? Where was the justice in this!

The next day, Sunday, the answer came. God in his mercy had not forgotten us.

The President of the PTA called me up. "Rivka, you can stop worrying. Shimmy is being readmitted, and the Principal will probably call you himself to let you know. I didn't want you to suffer unnecessarily for even five minutes, so I quickly called you."

"What happened?" I asked, shocked.

"Listen, when the PTA heard what had happened, we called Rabbi Brown and objected. As simple as that! It seems some rich parent made a whole fuss and demanded that your son be thrown out. But when Gila (the fifth mother in the car pool) heard, she called me, and told me how sweet your son is and how he has improved so much from the beginning of the year. So, to make a long story short, we put pressure on Rabbi Brown."

"Oh, I just don't know how to thank you! Thank you so much! Thank you! Thank you!" I repeated.

It was unbelievable! I was overjoyed for Shimmy. I was grateful that I would not have to tell him that he could not go to school anymore. But one phone call could not just turn off all emotion. There were bitter feelings that were not so easily erased. I phoned the members of my car pool to tell them that Shimmy was going to school on Monday. In particular I called to thank Gila. There was suddenly nothing to do or feel except gratefulness that for now I had a school where I could send Shimmy.

It was during this critical time that Dr. Gillman had pronounced those words to me: "Why don't you start your own school?"

At the time that he had said this, I was emotionally drained, and annoyed by the suggestion. But the idea was not totally cast aside, only temporarily buried.

6

THE NEXT FEW MONTHS passed uneventfully, a blessed relief after the first half of that school year. When the neurologist next saw Shimmy he gave us a new recommendation: Shimmy should be tested by a psychologist. He still could not point to any definite neurological disorder and although Shimmy had definitely improved, he was still noticeably delayed both in speech and fine motor coordination. Further testing was warranted.

I met with the psychologist who once again went through the whole routine of questions. She explained that she would spread the testing over three sessions, because of Shimmy's young age and short attention span. This way he would have the maximum opportunity to show his ability.

I took Shimmy to the first session — and during those forty-five minutes, he demanded to be taken to the bathroom eight times! For the second session, Yehoshua accompanied him. The psychologist noted that Shimmy was somewhat more responsive to his father than he was to me, and that is true. In fact, to this day he listens to Yehoshua without hesitation. He does not take me so seriously!

The psychologist called us for a meeting and evaluation after only two sessions. I remember saying to Yehoshua on the drive there, "I keep hoping that when we get there she will just say, 'Listen, all this testing has been done for nothing. There is nothing wrong with your Shimmy. He is a cute little boy who is just speaking a little late.' Don't you think it is possible, Yehoshua? He *seems* normal. Everyone who comes to our house finds him so cute and friendly."

Yehoshua sighed. "It is possible, Rivka. But don't count on it."

The psychologist, Mrs. Peters, sat down behind her desk. She began to review the testing results. "At the beginning, Shimmy performed well and eagerly. However, as the tasks grew progressively more difficult he began to try and avoid them. He asked to go to the bathroom frequently. He would not remain seated." She broke down the different parts of the test and in finishing her assessment, she informed us that Shimmy's IQ was 66, and fell in the mildly retarded range.

Retarded! That word was so ugly, so shocking, so devastating. That my son might be *retarded* was something I had never let myself acknowledge, as even the slightest possibility. Neither Yehoshua nor I said anything to Dr. Peters. We seemed to have turned to stone.

"Would you like to meet again to discuss this?" she asked politely.

I could not imagine, at the time, whatever for! What more was there to say? *Retarded!*

Yehoshua found words. "No, thank you."

And we left. I remember the first thing I said when I got into the car. I remember it distinctly, because I often felt guilty afterwards that that was my first reaction. "Let's not tell anyone," I said, and then, my usual exclamation: "I cannot believe it! Maybe it's all a mistake. Remember when he picked up the branch from the yard and pretended it was a flute? He went toot-toot and the two little boys from next door imitated him. That shows he has imagination. A child with such imagination cannot be re...slow. Maybe she just doesn't know what she's talking about — just like Dr. Gillman didn't, when he said Shimmy was deaf. What do you think?"

Yehoshua, at the time, seemed quite calm. "I think she is probably right," he said softly. "I think it is probably true."

Neither of us could say the word *retarded*. To this day I seldom use it.

I prefer the terminology "developmentally delayed," the words the neurologist had used as a possible explanation for Shimmy's not talking. But then I had not really understood what they signified. Literally, "developmentally delayed" means someone whose developmental growth has been slowed down. Somehow the implication to me was that this was a temporary condition. It somehow sounds hopeful. Surely a child who is delayed can catch up! *Retarded* sounds so final — so unchanging, so hopeless.

At the time Yehoshua and I did not really know how to react or proceed. What comes next? What do we do with Shimmy now? The one thing we knew was that we wanted him to continue in the nursery of Torah Academy for that year. We would not tell the school anything. The following year was a big uncertainty.

Since then, I have read many books and articles, attended workshops and lectures. And I have learned and corrected a misconception: IQ's *can* change. There is no black and white, "retarded" and "not retarded." Rather there is a spectrum, a curve, and people — human beings — span the arc from profoundly retarded to genius. In the middle are those who are "normal." And of the normal there are those who are high normal, brighter than average, and there are those who are normal, your everyday person who may, with much effort, get a college degree.

Within the range "below normal" there are different levels

also — and Shimmy was within the high educably retarded range. Below that are the retarded who can be trained to perform certain tasks, and subsequently can be trained for certain vocations. There are lower levels as well.

While it is very difficult to determine a definite diagnosis on young children, it helps to evaluate them to see what are their areas of strength and weakness. A qualified special educator can then utilize the strengths to improve the problem areas. But to affix a label on a child serves no purpose. The terms "retarded," "minimal brain dysfunction," "learning disabled," "attention deficit syndrome," or "autistic" do not help. In fact they are often discarded when another possible diagnosis presents itself in their place. Children are able to move up the spectrum.

7

AFTER THE FIRST few days, as the shock began to wear off, I began once again worrying about what Shimmy would do next year. I did not worry about what would be in ten years, or when he grew up. For me the immediate future was enough of a serious concern, and I was certain of one thing: Torah Academy would not be willing to accept him for another year.

I called up the OT to ask her when her next meeting with Shimmy would be, and also to ask her for information about the three-day special educational school she had previously recommended. I was quite surprised when, after she gave me the name and phone number I requested, she informed me that she did not think it worthwhile for her to continue to work with Shimmy any longer — "...since you are not following my recommendations." She was curt.

When I hung up the phone, I felt that we — Shimmy and I — had been abandoned. I suspected that she had learned the results of Shimmy's psychological testing and had decided that it was simply not worth her while to bother with him any longer. I was terribly hurt. Did she feel Shimmy was hopeless?

I felt bitter, too. No one cared. No one could help us!

It was at this time, a few weeks before Passover, that my older sister and her husband, who live in Carlton, invited us to come to them for the holiday. We were happy to have the opportunity to spend Passover together, and it was nice to think of all the cousins becoming reacquainted — for my second sister also lives in Carlton. At the same time, my brother-in-law informed Yehoshua that he had heard of a position opening up in the Yeshiva Day School in Carlton. Rabbi Fine was looking for a Rebbe for the high school and a dormitory supervisor. Benny, my sister's husband, had recommended Yehoshua for the position and Rabbi Fine was very interested.

In fact, only two days later, Rabbi Fine called up Yehoshua in Canada and arranged to interview him during our Pesach visit.

At the time of my sister's call, I was just beginning to reconcile myself to Shimmy's diagnosis. I told her vaguely that it was found that Shimmy had some learning difficulties and that I was looking for a preschool for him for the following year. She had encouraging information: There was a wonderful preschool in Carlton, she said, called Children's Educational Center, geared primarily to children with emotional and behavioral problems. The teachers work with the children on an individual basis, and a low student-teacher ratio is maintained. It sounded very good. True, Shimmy's primary problem was not emotional, but because of his frustration at not being able to communicate well, he still acted out aggressively. We arranged to visit Children's Educational Center when we came to Carlton.

We as Orthodox Jews believe that everything that happens is God's will and is ultimately for the good. It was evident to us that Providence was showing us new possibilities.

Yehoshua was offered the position in Carlton, and Children's Educational Center was willing to accept Shimmy. The details of his enrollment, such as tuition and transportation, were left to be discussed later.

Back in Canada, Yehoshua and I discussed the pros and cons of the move. The job of dormitory supervisor entailed our living in an apartment in the dormitory on the school's campus. Thus while our rent would be free, our privacy would be limited. Moreover, there were only a few Jewish families in the immediate neighborhood, and living in the dormitory would make socializing difficult for the children.

On the positive side, Yosef could easily walk to school and there was a car pool for Chaya to the girls' school. The apartment was large and roomy. Financially, even if I did not work, we would be doing better. And there was also a good chance I would be able to get a teaching position in Carlton. The Canadian dollar had gone down in value, but our debt remained in American dollars. We had paid back a little over half of our debt by then and had found it increasingly difficult to manage financially in Canada.

For me personally, leaving Canada meant leaving a very satisfying teaching position. It had taken me several months and the production of the first school play to gain the friendship and respect of my students. I often had disciplinary problems when teaching but once I had won the students over on a personal level they then seemed to agree to be good in class too. I had worked hard in preparation for my Bible and Prophets classes and felt that I was doing a good job teaching the 7th, 8th, 9th and 10th graders. The thought of having to start all over again in a new school troubled me. We had already made four major moves in our married life and I was concerned about the strain of having to adjust once again. However, I told myself, with my two sisters there already, we would not be coming as total strangers.

The decision was not as hard for Yehoshua, since the position was very appealing, both financially and professionally. Being the dormitory supervisor would introduce him to administrative experience.

Finally, of course, a strong argument for going was the

existence of a good school for Shimmy. Though it was a private, secular school, it sounded ideal for him.

The school year came to an end, and we sadly said goodbye to our friends. Yehoshua and I would both miss our many students. Coincidentally, two families who were our close friends were also leaving that year for new positions. None of us would miss the hard, cold winters.

We returned to the bungalow colony for the summer. I contacted the Carlton Girls' School and was very relieved when I learned I would have a teaching position there. We needed the money for the debt, and I knew myself: I would need to be busy in order to adjust to a new city.

8

MY SISTERS WELCOMED us to Carlton and we began to settle in. Yosef entered second grade in Hebrew Academy. Chaya began first grade. I shared a babysitter for Yona with another mother who taught in the Jewish girls' school.

Shortly after moving into our dormitory apartment, we learned that Children's Educational Center was not going to be the answer for Shimmy. It turned out that we lived right past the border of Carlton city — and were residents of Carlton county. The Center was in Carlton city. The county and city each had separate schooling and educational financing. Carlton county would not subsidize Shimmy's education in a city school unless they had no existing suitable program. Also, never would a public school bus cross the county line to transport a county child to a city school. Since both Yehoshua and I would be working, we would not have the time to drive him to school or pick him up. The cost of the special school, plus the cost of arranging transportation, was prohibitive to us at that time.

It was quite a disappointment, since we had felt so confident that Children's Educational Center would be the right place for Shimmy. But we did not despair, and we learned through my sister that the county had its own school — Fredericks School — that was similar to Children's Educational Center. It had an excellent diagnostic preschool that continued through the elementary level, and it was geared to children with learning disabilities, with or without accompanying emotional problems. However, we needed a referral.

My sister highly recommended her pediatrician, Dr. Glick, a warm, friendly, middle-aged man. I came with Shimmy's records and asked for his intervention in getting Shimmy into Fredericks School. Dr. Glick was charmed with Shimmy, who shook his hand when they met. He gave me the number to call and he himself wrote a letter recommending placement for Shimmy in a special educational kindergarten, putting into motion the accepted procedure for children with disabilities.

(There are many laws in the United States that were enacted to guarantee the right of all children to receive an education. The famous law, Public Law 94-142, was passed on Nov. 20, 1975: The Education for All Handicapped Children Act, considered the Bill of Rights for children with learning disabilities and other handicaps. In conjunction to this law, there are "child find" centers whose purpose is to locate very young children with handicaps. For it is a basic principle that the earlier the child receives aid, the quicker the rate of improvement. It is also important to help these young children from an emotional point of view, to prevent frustrations which result from their disabilities and the consequent development of a poor self-image. It has also proven to be cost-effective to help the child when he is younger, for he can learn to compensate for difficulties or even to overcome them early and thus the years necessary for providing special education can be cut in half.)

I was asked to send all Shimmy's records from Canada to Fredericks School. These records included the reports from the ear, nose and throat doctor, the speech therapist, occupational therapist, neurologist and psychologist, with the IQ results.

The secretary of Fredericks telephoned me shortly afterwards to inform me that Fredericks was not an appropriate placement for Shimmy, and they were therefore referring him to the Green Fields diagnostic nursery school. Once again I felt let down and rejected by professionals. I was determined to be calm about this new development.

In the meantime, we were tremendously relieved when Rabbi Fine granted Shimmy admission to Hebrew Academy's morning nursery. Shimmy would be three quarters of a year older than the other children, but that was fine. He was excited about the opportunity to go to nursery school again. He loved it and could not wait to start.

I called up Shana Nathan, my friend Deenie's sister, who was a special education teacher in the Carlton city public school system. I felt she would answer me truthfully as to what type of school Green Fields was.

"As far as I remember," she told me, "it is basically a school for severely handicapped children. But if they are recommending this place to you, then they must have a diagnostic kindergarten or something. You will just have to go down and see for yourself."

Yehoshua agreed that we would have to go and see what the school was like before we made any decision. Though the principal was on sick leave, we made an appointment to see the school the following morning. Yehoshua took time off from work and we took Shimmy along with us. As we sat in the hall waiting for the assistant principal to come out and show us around, I found I was becoming more and more apprehensive about sending Shimmy to this school. First, a teacher walked by escorting a child with a walker. An aide wheeled another little boy down the hall in a wheelchair. Then a line of five noticeably retarded students, accompanied by their teacher, went down the hall. Where were the children like Shimmy?

An attractive young woman approached us and smiled. She

addressed Shimmy first. "Hi! What's your name?"

"Shimmy," he answered with a smile.

I saw her perplexed expression and explained, "Shimmy, short for Shimon — Simon. It's a Hebrew name. Do you teach here?" I asked.

"Yes, I teach older, severely handicapped, children — not like your son." Here she seemed to catch herself. "Though, we do have a program for younger children who are higher functioning."

Just then Mr. Park, a pink-faced man, fiftyish, with a smooth bald head came over to us. I think it was the shallow look in his eyes and his foolish grin which immediately made a poor impression on both Yehoshua and me.

"Sorry to have kept you waiting. It's a pity that Dr. Gabel was not able to come, but I will be happy to show you the three morning classes of our diagnostic kindergarten. Of course, none of these are appropriate for your son, since you requested an afternoon program. However, these classes are similar to the afternoon classes." He kept up a steady chatter as he lead us down the hall. We passed a beautiful gym, a well-equipped room for physical therapy and several classrooms. We came to the first diagnostic kindergarten, and walked in. My stomach felt like it dropped! I felt sick.

There were six children altogether. Three were in wheelchairs; two had Down's Syndrome; and the sixth child was sitting with a vacant look in his eyes. The teacher had given them musical instruments and was trying to lead them in a song.

"And you think Shimmy belongs here?" I asked incredulously.

"Oh, this is just one of our classes," he smoothly replied, totally insensitive to my reaction. "Come, let us go next door."

The next room contained another group of children who once again gave the impression of being much lower functioning than Shimmy. A cute little black boy gave us a big friendly smile and said "Hello."

We smiled back, a bit encouraged, and answered "Hello."

The third class was similar to the previous two. About two thirds of the children were visibly handicapped. That friendly little boy was the only one who, like Shimmy, did not look retarded or disabled.

Over the years I have learned that one cannot judge intelligence by physical appearance — a child with cerebral palsy may be spastic yet have a brilliant mind. The features of a child with Down's Syndrome label him immediately as different, as retarded, yet when given proper stimulation and education a child with Down's Syndrome can attain an IQ within normal range. Children born with cleft palates may take longer to learn to speak and until they undergo many corrective operations appear unusual, yet basically their potential can be equal to the rest of the population.

Yehoshua's and my reaction to the children with severe disabilities in that school was thus due partly to ignorance, and partly to denial — to our refusal to accept that our child might be truly handicapped, as these children were, and partly to the foolish way Mr. Park took us around. If these classes contained children who were lower functioning than Shimmy, why show them to us? For us as parents it was very upsetting. It was as if Shimmy were being labeled. (Shimmy himself was mostly bored. He was not enjoying the tour at all, and just wanted to get out of this school.)

At any rate, our overwhelming reaction was that we wanted to leave immediately. We could not believe that anyone could think our Shimmy belonged with those children. They appeared to us as being empty and lifeless. And hopeless. The suggestion that Shimmy belonged with children like this was a terrible shock to us. It filled me with anger and sorrow.

Once again I called Shana for information. She explained to me that one part of the law guarantees handicapped children what is called "the least restrictive environment." This means loosely that it is a child's right to be taught in a class where he can learn according to his ability, but at the highest level in which he can function. For example, a child who cannot walk but who has normal intelligence should be allowed to attend a regular public school — even if it means that the school has to put in special ramps for his wheelchair. Such a child should not be placed in a school for the retarded simply because that school may already have ramps.

For us, this meant that a child with learning disabilities like Shimmy's should not be placed in a class with children who are even moderately retarded. Though Shimmy's IQ was below normal, we refused to equate our friendly, personable little boy with children so obviously handicapped.

I was angry that Mr. Park had so blandly indicated these classes as being appropriate for Shimmy. I was determined to get Shimmy into Fredericks. Once again I contacted Dr. Glick, who requested that Shimmy be re-evaluated in order to determine appropriate placement, since we, the parents, felt that Green Fields was not suitable.

Fredericks School is part of the Carlton county evaluation center. Shimmy received an extensive evaluation once again, free of charge. His hearing test revealed a very minor hearing loss; the speech and psychological tests placed him once again in the mildly retarded range. I did not have confidence in the psychologist since she seemed to me to immediately form an impression of Shimmy based on the former test results she had read. At the outset of the testing, when Shimmy showed reluctance to enter the room alone, she had commented, "I suspect I will find much the same as the doctor in Canada found." How could she say such a thing! Indeed she seemed to triumphantly declare at the end of the two sessions of testing, "It looks like I was right — his IQ has not improved at all."

I was heartsick at her pronouncement. I did not like Dr. Mead, did not trust her, and did not want to believe her. All the same, I realized that even if she were off a bit in her scoring, it did seem to be true that Shimmy definitely did not have a normal IQ.

When, two weeks later, we got a call to attend a meeting at Fredericks about placement for Shimmy I insisted that Yehoshua accompany me. I wanted him to persuade the "team" that Green Fields was not the "least restrictive environment" to which our son was entitled.

The team consisted of the principal of Green Fields, the principal of Fredericks, the psychologist and perhaps one or two more of the testers, and the speech or occupational therapists. Yehoshua and I felt outnumbered by "experts." And although Yehoshua had reacted as I had to the tour of Green Fields, the latest IQ test made him feel unsure of our position. Still, we maintained that Green Fields was not the "least restrictive environment."

At the meeting, Mrs. Thomas, principal of Fredericks, presided. After briefly reviewing the test results and the recommendation for Shimmy to attend Green Fields, she turned to us and said, "Based on these reports, it seems that Shimon would definitely not be suitable for Fredericks. We cannot accept him. Green Fields has an excellent diagnostic kindergarten for children of his ability."

I began to protest. "But I do not believe that Shimmy has such limited ability. He is not *really* retarded. The classes we saw at Green Fields had children with blank expressions, children who were obviously handicapped. Who could Shimmy talk to? Who would talk to him — so that he could learn to talk properly?" I felt desperate for them to consider this point.

Dr. Gabel, principal of Green Fields, turned to Yehoshua and me, and spoke in a kindly tone. "Rabbi and Mrs. Walburg, I apologize for not being able to greet you when you came to the school. Unfortunately, you did not see the class we have in mind for your son — the afternoon class definitely has children whose problems are more similar to Shimon's. Mr. Park just wanted you to see the size of the classes, the equipment, and the general setup. In our diagnostic kindergarten, we seek to find the strengths of the children and utilize them, while working to compensate for their weakness. I think you will find it quite appropriate for Shimon. While the teachers work with the children, they observe and recommend whatever further assistance a child may require. Why don't you and your husband come one afternoon and observe the particular class we recommend for Shimon."

Yehoshua and I saw we had little choice but to comply. Fredericks was obviously closed to Shimmy.

The next afternoon we arrived at Green Fields. Dr. Gabel took us straight to Miss Baxter's class, and there to our surprise and relief we saw four cute little girls and one little boy, sitting around a small table, each coloring a circle red. Miss Baxter immediately invited Shimmy to sit down and join the other children, and he happily did so. She gave him a paper and a red crayon. Shimmy looked at us questioningly and I hurried to reassure him.

Dr. Gabel introduced us to the children. One little girl, Patty, was in a wheelchair, but she had a sweet lively face encircled by curly blond hair. Dr. Gabel explained that this little girl had undergone surgery for a brain tumor at age one and a half! She was now recovering the use of most of her body, but still could not walk and needed a small group and individual attention. She was frail but seemed quite alert and intelligent.

Timothy, the little boy, had Down's Syndrome but I was surprised to hear him speaking fairly well. Another little girl, Lydia, reminded me of Shimmy: she was friendly and very communicative, but her speech was a bit garbled like his. She also seemed to have a short attention span. Dr. Gabel told us a little about Lydia. She was the only child of an older couple who had been thrilled when she was born. When they began to become concerned about her delayed speech and ultimately had her tested, they were devastated. Their long-awaited child was not the perfect bundle of joy they had yearned for. Dr. Gabel knew the parents personally and had understood their sorrow. He helped them adjust to their sweet but less-than-perfect child and he had guided them into placing her in Green Fields.

Yehoshua and I were impressed with his telling us this personal story. We could see that he was a sympathetic and compassionate person. And we understood he was gently telling us that we too were having a normal reaction to learning that our son had a handicap. We too, like Lydia's devastated parents, would have to accept reality and deal with it.

In the meantime Shimmy was having a wonderful time with Miss Baxter. Both Yehoshua and I sensed that we were in the presence of a talented, caring teacher. We looked at each other and I turned to Dr. Gabel. "Okay," I said, smiling.

It took a few days and transportation was arranged. Shimmy continued going to the Hebrew Academy nursery in the morning, and at noon a bus picked him up from there, took him to Green Fields, and returned him at 3:30. The arrangement worked out pretty well. Shimmy got some exposure to basic preschool Jewish education in the mornings, including the prayers and songs which he loved. And in the afternoons, Miss Baxter worked with him on colors, shapes and basic concepts that average children just pick up from their environment. Shimmy needed to be taught and retaught basic concepts such as: big and small, in and out, up and down, in front and in back, etc. He also had a session with a speech therapist once a week.

This was the first time Shimmy had attended a non-Jewish school. At the beginning I explained to Miss Baxter that we were Orthodox Jews, and only kosher food could be given to our son. Since even the serving of snacks involved the teaching of basic skills, Miss Baxter provided me with a weekly schedule so that I could ensure that Shimmy's snacks were kosher. Instead of Shimmy eating the jello they prepared in school, I would make green or red kosher jello and send it along with him. He could eat fruit from the school but any cooked or baked products I would send from home. I also explained that the little skullcap on his head — the *kippah* — and the fringes under his shirt — his *tzitzis*, were religious articles of clothing that all Jewish boys must wear. Miss Baxter was very understanding, and subsequently explained the *kippah* and *tzitzis* to the other children.

Shimmy went happily each day, and Yehoshua and I accepted his going to Green Fields. We had no choice.

9

IT WAS NOT until the beginning of March, when we celebrated the Festival of Purim, that we began to feel that we were not providing Shimmy with all that he needed. Purim is an extremely joyous holiday, commemorating the deliverance of the Jews of Persia from the massacre plotted by the evil Haman. Yosef and Chaya had been very excited for weeks in advance, planning their costumes and constantly changing their minds about what they would be: a clown, the wicked Haman, the hero Mordechai, the heroine Queen Esther. They looked forward to hearing the story read aloud from a scroll in the synagogue, and to sending neighbors and friends baskets of fruit and cakes. In our family, we all — grownups as well as children — dress up in costumes, and from the time we were married Yehoshua and I have always invited between twenty and fifty guests to join us in our holiday feast. It is the one time of year when liquor is liberally served and some drunkenness is even condoned.

That year, when Shimmy was four, Yosef dressed up as a clown and Chaya — like most little girls — chose to be Queen

Esther. Yehoshua borrowed a friend's long black coat and dressed up as a Chassid, while I braided a long red wig, put on a pinafore and striped knee socks, painted freckles on my face and was a Raggedy Ann of sorts. Even little Yona was made up to look like a clown. I tried to encourage Shimmy to join the fun and dress up too, but he refused all joyful attempts to put on a costume. It was upsetting to see a little boy so bewildered by the joy of Purim. He was very bothered to see his father wearing the long black satin coat. While all the children played and ate ice cream and cake at our festive meal, Shimmy simply climbed into bed and slept Purim away. He had found Purim very confusing. He had not grasped at all what was going on.

Despite the fact that in Hebrew Academy's nursery the teachers had told the story of Purim, and the children had made masks and colorful paper baskets, Shimmy just did not understand what it was all about. It was sad that he could not enjoy the holiday most loved by Jewish children.

I had prepared several dozen *hamentashen*, triangular jelly-filled cookies traditionally eaten on Purim. I sent a bag of them to Green Fields with Shimmy and a note to the teacher, explaining that these cookies were to be shared with the class, in the spirit of our Jewish holiday, Purim.

Somehow the teacher never saw the note, and the cookies were stored in Shimmy's cubby, to be used as kosher snacks for him. She had not understood, and neither had he. I learned this two months later.

When Easter came shortly afterwards and Shimmy brought home colored cut-out bunnies, I could not get too enthused about them. Shimmy did not know that we, as Jews, do not celebrate Easter and the accompanying customs.

These two incidents so close together made me suddenly realize that special education was not enough. For a child from a religious family like ours, special education would have to be in a religious environment. Shimmy's Jewish education was being neglected.

10

WE WENT TO NEW YORK to celebrate Pesach with my parents that year. They were pleased to see that Shimmy was becoming much more verbal and my father was especially proud of Shimmy's decorum in the synagogue.

Shimmy enjoyed sitting with his *Zaidie*, his grandfather, and kept his *siddur* open throughout the service. He would join the singing wherever it was appropriate; he knew to answer *Amen* and the proper responses in *Kaddish* and a few other prayers. After the prayers, Shimmy made a point of going around and shaking hands with all the men, determinedly approaching the older Rabbis with great respect and loudly exclaiming, "*Good Shabbos! Good Yom Tov!*"

It is no wonder that everyone knew and appreciated this little boy who so accurately imitated their own behavior, even wishing them a happy Sabbath and Holiday. The other children were quick to discern Shimmy's popularity with their parents, and became very friendly towards him as well.

At the Passover Seder, Shimmy sang the first question of the traditional Four Questions in Hebrew. His articulation was imperfect; his younger cousin Avi knew all four of the questions, but we cheered them equally for their efforts. Shimmy went to sleep early.

Two weeks later was the annual Torah Umesorah Convention, a gathering of educators from Jewish day schools and yeshivas throughout North America. That year it was held in upstate New York. Yehoshua's participation was sponsored by his school, and we decided that I too would attend, for the first time.

We left Carlton on Friday morning, dropping Shimmy and Yosef off with my parents; the other two children were left with my sisters in Carlton. The convention took place in a homey, kosher hotel in the Catskill Mountains. I found the whole weekend to be a spiritually uplifting experience as well as an enjoyable vacation. Famous Rabbis and prestigious Jewish professionals spoke on interesting topics and were very inspiring, and being away at a hotel by ourselves was a welcome change.

The highlight of the weekend was our meeting and talking to Rabbi Dr. A. H. Fried. Rabbi Fried, a brilliant psychologist and innovative educator, is the champion of Jewish children with learning disabilities. While serving as Principal of a *cheder*, he founded the first special education class in such a school. In this traditional ultra-Orthodox elementary school for boys, Rabbi Dr. Fried introduced many progressive methods in the teaching of religious subjects. His *cheder* became famous and grew as parents from many Chassidic sects sought the best school for their children.

One day a parent approached Rabbi Dr. Fried, pleading for his child's acceptance into the *cheder*. This child had learning problems and had already been expelled from two *cheder*s. The family was ultra-Orthodox and desperate to see their son placed only in a religious environment. They viewed public school as a devastating option.

In order to appreciate the enormity of the problem, it should be pointed out that the *cheder* program is geared for bright children and is quite accelerated. A child with learning disabilities will soon find it very difficult keeping up with his classmates, and this initiates a vicious circle: Because of his disabilities, the child encounters failure; this makes him more and more discouraged, his self-image plummets, emotional problems often develop as a result, and ultimately he will become either the class clown, the class troublemaker, the class introvert, or simply depressed.

This is the scenario of most children with learning disabilities, whether in private or public school, but children in American Jewish schools face an even greater hurdle, since they have a dual curriculum: secular subjects and religious subjects. They are required to learn to read and write not one, but two languages: Hebrew or Yiddish, which goes from right to left, and English, which goes from left to right. For the child whose specific disability involves reading, this can be extremely confusing, if not disastrous.

It has been found, however, that once a child begins to learn to overcome or compensate for his difficulty, he will progress in other areas as well. Thus many of these children are able to master the two languages when given the proper attention.

Rabbi Dr. Fried had assured the distraught parents that he would help them find a suitable school for their son. But after making numerous phone calls, he discovered the sad truth that there was no place for the learning-disabled Jewish boy. This little boy, as well as other Jewish learning-disabled children, could become lost souls! Jewish day schools, *cheders*, and yeshivas were not equipped with knowledge, methods, facilities or staff to deal with the problem child.

Rabbi Dr. Fried felt he had to keep his promise to the parents. He opened up the first special education class in his own *cheder*. As word of this class spread, applicants began swarming to his office. Through great luck — or, as we believe, Divine intervention — a Jewish company with excess office space was able to provide room for Rabbi Fried's "new" school.

Rabbi Fried, in addition to establishing this wonderful

special education school in Brooklyn, also founded a similar school in Jerusalem, and ultimately helped establish programs in England, Canada and various cities in the United States and Europe.

When Yehoshua and I first approached this famous man, I was overawed. Here we were about to talk to this innovator and founder, brilliant lecturer, doctor of psychology and respected Rabbi — all rolled into one tall red-headed Chassid.

Making the first overture, Yehoshua extended his hand. "*Shalom aleichem.* I am Yehoshua Walburg. Can you spare a few minutes to speak to my wife and me?"

Graciously, Rabbi Dr. Fried led us to a small cluster of chairs in the lobby and asked us to join him.

Yehoshua began, "We have a four-and-a-half-year old son whom we suspect has learning disabilities. His IQ test puts him in the slightly below normal range."

I continued with the description of Shimmy, and told him how he attended Hebrew Academy of Carlton in the mornings and went to a public special education school in the afternoons. Our main concern, I explained, was our feeling that he needed more direction in order to understand his Jewish identity. After all, he was almost five. "Should we continue sending him to a public school half a day and to the Jewish kindergarten? I do not think he will be able to get much out of next year's kindergarten program in Hebrew Academy — it will be beyond him. Should we move to New York to send him to your school?"

Rabbi Dr. Fried turned to me, and answered tersely, an answer that echoed the advice of old Dr. Gillman: "*Start your own school.*"

This time I laughed. "*I*? How could *I* start a school? I don't know anything about special education. And I don't know anything about starting schools!"

"I am absolutely serious, Mrs. Walburg. And I will help you. Are you willing to organize a public meeting in Carlton? Ask the Jewish schools to jointly sponsor my trip to Carlton, and publicize an open meeting for the purpose of exploring special education and the Jewish learning-disabled child. I will be pleased to come and speak. You can note the names of all those who attend and thus you will have your first mailing list. These people will be the base for founding and organizing a school. It's important to arrange this meeting very soon, for the school year is almost over and there isn't much time until the new year starts."

His enthusiasm was contagious and I was caught up in it. "Okay! I'll arrange the meeting as soon as possible and we will take it from there. I'll be in touch with you next week to confirm a definite date. Thank you so much."

I enjoyed everything about that convention, but from the moment I had spoken to this great man, I could only think of one thing: setting up this meeting in Carlton. My mind was racing with ideas. With great excitement I acted upon his suggestion immediately, before the convention was over. The principals of three out of four of Carlton's Jewish schools were also attending.

First I broached the suggestion to Rabbi Fine of our Hebrew Academy. His response was encouraging: He himself had a nephew with some learning difficulty, he told me, and he was certainly interested in learning more about the subject. After such a positive response from him, I had the courage to approach the principal of the girls' school, and the principal of the Carlton *cheder*. Their agreement so encouraged me that I was "high" that whole weekend. Something very special was going to happen! I knew it! When I returned home I spoke to the principal of the remaining school, a modern Jewish day school. He was willing to participate with the other three schools. That the four Jewish elementary schools of Carlton would jointly sponsor a lecture was in itself a good omen.

"It's amazing," I told Yehoshua. "When I first heard the suggestion from Dr. Gillman I rejected the idea, and now it seems actually feasible!"

11

THE MEETING WAS SET for May 28th. With the help of my sister and several friends, fliers were sent to all the parents of the four Jewish schools, and a notice was also placed in the local paper. In addition to giving his lecture, Rabbi Dr. Fried agreed to remain until the following night to help us formally set up an organization.

Over 200 people attended the lecture, which took place in Hebrew Academy's lunchroom. Among those were educational administrators, both secular and religious teachers, psychologists, various therapists, and last but not least, parents of children with sundry handicaps.

Rabbi Dr. Fried held the attention of this large, diverse crowd for over two-and-a half hours! Using many different audio-visual aids, including a projector and slide show of his special *cheder* in Williamsburg, he was able to teach everyone something, and many learned much. It was a happening! I was exhilarated by the whole evening, and when Rabbi Fried announced that the following evening there would be a meeting for those interested in participating in the formation of a group in Carlton for learning-disabled children, I could hardly believe it.

The following night, May 29th, about one tenth of the previous nights' crowd attended the follow-up meeting. Under Rabbi Fried's guidance, we voted to create a PTACH chapter in Carlton. PTACH, the Hebrew imperative for "Open!", is an acronym for Parents for Torah for All Children. It was originally a parent support group started in New York by parents of children with learning disabilities, and Rabbi Dr. Fried was one of the original advisors. Although he himself was no longer affiliated with the organization, he encouraged us to establish our group with an easily recognizable identity. By formalizing our group it would facilitate our starting educational programs.

In forming this organization, he pointed out, there were several steps necessary. We had to clearly define our goals and basic philosophy; and in order to start a special education class, we had to document the need. To this end, Rabbi Dr. Fried asked those present with problem children to fill out a short questionnaire, so we could get an idea of the needs of the population.

He also explained to those educators present the concept of the resource class, a classroom in an ordinary school used for providing special help and attention for those children who require it. A special education teacher meets with the children individually, or in small groups during the regular school day, for short sessions of between twenty minutes and an hour. For example, a child with dyslexia — literally, the inability to read — may be taught with a method totally different from the one used in the regular class. Instead of teaching first the ABC and then phonetically building a word (b-a-t = bat), a child like this may find it easier to learn the whole word: bat. Other children can even be taught with the same methods used in their regular class, but because of their high level of distractibility, they may simply need the individual attention in a quiet setting to help them initially master a skill.

Resource help like this is for the child who, for the most part, can remain in the regular classroom. He leaves his homeroom for a short period to overcome specific disabilities, during which time he is taught to compensate for weakness and to build up his skill. Skills are broken down into a hierarchy of tasks. Learning is building knowledge. One fact or skill can provide the base for the next one. We learn to count before we can add; we learn to add before we can multiply. With special education, the steps are smaller but the goals are the same as those of other children. Finally, Rabbi Dr. Fried asked the principals present if they saw a need for such a program in their schools.

"Definitely!" Rabbi Fine from Hebrew Academy promptly replied. "In fact, several candidates come to mind immediately." The Rabbi from Beth Jacob and the Rabbi from the Carlton *cheder* remained quiet.

But nothing would stop me now, and I took the initiative. "What about the girls' school, Rabbi Goldman?" I asked.

"Oh, no!" he hastened to assure all those present. "We have no problem students whatsoever."

Rabbi Wolf of the *cheder* must have felt my stare upon him. He looked up and announced quietly, "The Carlton *cheder* has no need for a special program. We have only very bright students."

I knew that both these principals were mistaken, and at the time I was very annoyed by their stand. Was it pride that did not let them see reality? From the very first day that I had begun publicizing the meeting, I had been besieged by phone calls from concerned parents. One mother of a six-year-old called me, greatly upset. "I am so glad you are calling this meeting, Rivka. You do not know what I have been through: My Rachel is going to have to attend a Christian private school next year, as she has been totally miserable in the girls' school, and I have no alternative. She cannot read and only recently, last month, we found out that her problem is due to poor vision. She is very farsighted and no one ever suspected it. All year, her teachers made her feel like a dummy because she couldn't read."

Though I was disturbed by this story, somehow I did not wholly believe all the details. Somehow I had a sense that the mother's great despair in learning that she had a child with a problem had colored her perception of what was going on in school with Rachel. By now my own experience had taught me this. However, knowing even part of Rachel's story proved to me that Rabbi Goldman had not given an accurate account of his students' needs. Yet I had no definite proof with which to refute his statement.

We proceeded with the rest of the agenda — the next step was electing officers to meet and formulate goals, and to begin to work toward their fulfillment.

Nominations were open — and there was silence. No one nominated anyone! Looking around the room, everyone seemed to be avoiding my eyes. Once again I took the initiative. "I nominate myself vice-president!" I declared. Everyone laughed and voted me in.

Then, one mother who has bookkeeping skills volunteered to be treasurer. My friend Susanne Cohen volunteered to be secretary. And then there was silence again.

I felt myself becoming angry. "Listen, if no one else is interested in helping or being involved, why don't you all just go home! We are simply wasting time — I nominated myself *vice*-president, because I do not need honors. But I will work very hard with anyone, to get something started. Is anyone else interested in helping?" I demanded.

Rabbi Fried hastily intervened. "I suggest you elect a presidium, an executive committee of two, Rivka, and you be one of the presidents. Would anyone else agree to be part of a presidium?"

Quietly a young nursery school teacher volunteered. "I will be president with you, Rivka."

Rabbi Fried asked all present to vote the two of us in as a presidium. Now we were a real organization, with two presidents, a treasurer and a secretary.

Suddenly everyone began talking and milling about. Rabbi Fried had to catch a plane back to New York, and the meeting was adjourned without further ado.

I went home with a terribly nervous stomach, realizing that I had just made a major commitment. Until that time I had never even been involved formally in any organization — and certainly not on the management level. I did not sleep that night — or much any other night for several weeks. Besides the sudden influx of calls from parents like Rachel's mother, I was busy making follow-up calls from the list we had compiled at the first meeting. I still had a few weeks of teaching left; lessons had to be prepared; tests had to be made up and marked; report cards had to be filled out; and my four small children needed their mother too. Sleep was definitely my last priority.

12

THE DAY AFTER PTACH of Carlton came into existence, I called up Susanne Cohen with an urgent plea for help. Susanne is about ten years older than I, and she had served as secretary of several organizations in addition to working as a school secretary for several years. She is a mother of three. Her two younger children, a girl and a boy, are both active young adults, and each had excelled scholastically and socially in high school. Her oldest child, Benjamin, had difficulties.

His problems had begun with a difficult birth. But Susanne had been put to sleep during delivery and was not aware of what went on exactly. When he reached the end of his first year it was apparent that Benjamin was not developing at a normal rate. He was a very irritable baby and difficult to calm down. He began walking at a late age, and at age six he was barely speaking. Susanne had put him in a special school for the retarded. When after a year his teacher realized that Benjamin could tie his own shoes and had self-care skills on a level way above those of his classmates, she recommended his being placed into a higher functioning program. Susanne hired a speech therapist. She took Benjamin for physical therapy. She fought for acceptance into Hebrew Academy. She wanted her eight-year-old to receive a Jewish education.

There was much resistance. She and two other parents had tried at the time to start a special class but could not gain the cooperation of any of the existing schools, and so she had continued to provide Benjamin with private Hebrew lessons while sending him to public school. Benjamin, in turn, continued to learn and to progress, and his IQ — which had placed him in a very low functioning level at age 5-6 — rose until it reached a low normal range. Hebrew Academy accepted Benjamin, but he did not have an easy time of it. Nevertheless, his parents were grateful that he could be in a religious environment and learn about his heritage like any other Jewish child.

When Benjamin was born, fourteen years before Shimmy, the need for special education had not been acknowledged much in the secular world, and certainly not in the Jewish world. It was only after the first laws were passed in November 1975, that the concept of providing appropriate education for all children, including the handicapped, was accepted as obligatory.

Jewish special education came to the forefront even later. It was in 1976 that Rabbi Fried's first school was established, and prior to this few programs existed for Jewish handicapped children. I use the word "handicap" to encompass physical, mental and emotional problems.

I admired Susanne greatly. Not only was she an experienced secretary, a devoted mother, and a capable organizer, but she had managed to provide so much for her son without the benefit of assistance from an organization or the government. She remained kind and generous, and without bitter feelings. Now, she was very happy that finally the community was waking up to the realization that it was their responsibility to participate in the education of the handicapped Jewish child. Indeed she regretted that PTACH had not existed when her son so desperately needed help, and she was proud to be able to assist other children by being part of this vital organization.

When I called Susanne I was feeling very nervous and unsure of myself. "Susanne, thank you so much for agreeing to be secretary. But I must tell you that I do not know where to go from here! I know absolutely nothing about organizational structure."

"Calm down, Rivka," she said. "First, let's make a list of our short-term and long-term plans. If our goal is to start a special class, then let us determine what we need."

"Okay," I said, reaching for a pen and a pad and feeling better already. Somebody knew what to do! "To start a class we need, first of all, students. So I guess we have to get a professional to determine the needs in the school. Maybe we should put an advertisement in the paper saying PTACH is planning to open a class for children with learning disabilities, and all those interested should please contact me."

"Advertisements cost money, Rivka. And to start any school you need money for many things — especially for a teacher," said Susanne.

"A teacher! That would be number two on my list of what we need. Fortunately, Rabbi Fried already recommended one: Miriam Bender, an excellent special education teacher. She lives in Carlton, and her sister is Rabbi Fried's top teacher. He has met Miriam, had a favorable impression of her, and told me that if she's even only half as good as her sister Leah is, she would be excellent. So, I am not really worried about a teacher. I am also pretty confident that Rabbi Fine will give us classroom space in Hebrew Academy. That's the third item. So we are now up to the fourth item of our list — money. How do we get money?"

Susanne suggested we plan a meeting for the following Sunday, inviting the parents who expressed interest and the recently elected officers of our new PTACH group. Simultaneously, we should try to put together a meeting of professionals, for a professional advisory board would be crucial for a school for children with learning handicaps. Susanne and I reviewed the names of the professionals who had attended Rabbi Fried's lecture and we decided to try and call them all.

That same morning, Alice, a mother of a little boy Shimmy's age, was also in touch with me, and she recommended several other professionals who she felt would be an asset to our board.

I called Ellen Ganz, and she and Rena Stein, both child psychologists, refined Rabbi Fried's questionnaire and wrote an accompanying note. In essence we were asking parents if they had children diagnosed as handicapped, or whom they suspected had potential learning difficulties.

I phoned Shana Nathan and Miriam Bender and asked them to make an informal survey, to visit the Jewish schools and gain some impressions about the need for resource help. With the principals' support they would be able to get some idea, some number we could work from. However, to our disappointment, of the four Jewish schools, only Hebrew Academy agreed to this project. The principal of the modern day school informed me that they are very selective in accepting students, and do not have any children with problems. "And if we did have any," he said, "we would certainly provide for the needs of our students by ourselves."

Their attitude of superiority rankled. (Two years later, when I taught Bible classes there, I learned first hand that they did indeed have several students who had learning disabilities or were hyperactive.) The Rabbi of the *cheder* thanked us for our interest but stated they were already dealing with their problems. The administrators of the girls' school said that they were well acquainted with their student body, and at the present time they saw no need for anyone to investigate their needs in this respect. If they suspected problems in the future, they would then turn to PTACH for assistance.

We were left with Hebrew Academy, and even there Shana and Miriam did not gain the full cooperation of the teachers.

Despite this, and the fact that they had very few hours to conduct an adequate survey, they were nevertheless able to ascertain that there definitely existed several children with learning difficulties in Hebrew Academy.

The girls' school and Hebrew Academy ended their school terms in the middle of June. By July our family would be out of the city, in the bungalow colony, for once again Yehoshua had a position for the summer as a Rebbe. There was so little time and so much to do! I desperately wanted Shimmy to start an appropriate special class in September.

The phone became my constant companion. From early morning, while rushing to get everyone off to school, until midnight when I was finishing marking exams, I would have the phone set firmly between my shoulder and ear.

Yehoshua was very busy then with end-of-the-year preparations, as well as negotiating his contract for the following year. The board of Hebrew Academy had asked him to become the assistant principal of Hebrew Academy's high school. He would be in charge of the Jewish studies. This meant in effect that Yehoshua would come home to eat supper and then return to the school until late at night.

Our children were all being ignored to a certain extent, as PTACH became an absolute obsession for me. Though I continued my involvement for the full five years that we lived in Carlton, I never was as totally immersed as I was during those first five weeks. I even resorted to using television as a diversion for the children; I felt guilty but saw no other option. When we had first come to Carlton, we did not have a television, for Rabbi Fine had specifically informed Yehoshua that it would not be acceptable to have a television in the dormitory. However, an eye doctor in Carlton suggested that we permit Shimmy to watch television for a little while each day, as an exercise in focusing. At that point we went out and bought a small set that we kept hidden in our bedroom. Initially we permitted the children to view it only for short periods during the day. However, as time passed and I got busier, Yosef, Chaya and Shimmy would spend more and more time in front of the TV set. Even Yona would sit there spellbound. That June they set family records for hours of television viewed!

The first few days I was mostly involved with setting up and holding meetings. I borrowed from a neighbor *Robert's Rules of Order,* the classic work on parliamentary procedure. I needed to learn something about how to run a meeting, and it helped — but PTACH was not particularly strict about parliamentary procedure during my time. Though Judy Diamond had originally volunteered to be president along with me, it soon became clear that she would not be able to do so, for her husband had been offered an internship in Boston and they were preparing to leave Carlton. So I was left with the ultimate responsibility.

During the month of June, I was in contact with Rabbi Fried by long distance phone. Because he was very busy finishing up the school year in his two schools in New York, as well as in the process of starting a program in Jerusalem, he did not really have much time to help us in Carlton. Although he was very kind and always gave me advice when I was able to reach him, it became clear that PTACH of Carlton would need local professionals to deal with the many issues that came up.

One of his many suggestions was to contact the New York branch of PTACH and request literature from them, for if we were to become a branch we needed to follow their philosophy. I did so, and the president of PTACH in New York was excited at the expansion of the organization. They were already incorporated as a non-profit organization, I learned, and were willing to permit us to use their tax-exempt number.

The whole business of incorporating, tax rules, and legalities was an unknown subject to me, and I was suddenly forced to learn about many new areas.

A small meeting was held in our apartment for the purpose of determining the goals of PTACH. Susanne came and efficiently took minutes; several concerned mothers came, and it turned out that Alice and I were the only two who saw the establishment of a class as a necessity. We wanted a place for Shimmy and Barry, then, for the coming school year, and we were determined that it would become a reality. But we had differing opinions as to where the classroom should be situated.

I wanted the boys to be in the regular school building, in Hebrew Academy. This way they would have the opportunity to mingle with other children their age, even if only at recess. Alice felt strongly that the classroom should be in a separate building, and she knew of a synagogue that would provide classroom space for free. She was concerned that our children would be picked on and laughed at if they were in their own special class within a regular school.

The issue lead to a heated discussion. "I am not ashamed of Shimmy," I said. "I do not want to hide him away so no one will see him or meet him. I want him exposed to other children."

"You do not realize how cruel children can be," said Alice. "I know. It has happened more than enough times for my liking, that Barry has come home all upset, after having a fight with some boys. They tease him and make him angry, and he gets into terrible fights."

Mrs. Brunner, a retired principal and mother of an older handicapped child, tried to mediate. "While it is true that children can be cruel, they are only reflecting attitudes from home, you know. One of our tasks as an organization must be to educate the public. It is about time that other Jewish parents and Jewish schools come to accept our children. All Jewish children deserve acceptance."

No decision was formally reached. Although I felt strongly about this point, I realized it was certainly not worthwhile to cause a conflict at our first meeting. Trying to be diplomatic, I suggested, "Why don't we wait to come to a decision on this point. We have so many other things to resolve first."

"Let's just review our objectives and goals, both short and

long term," suggested Susanne quickly. "First of all we want to open a class in September, and a resource program, at least in Hebrew Academy. Secondly, we want to educate the public — including the teachers — about the nature of learning disabilities."

Though informally conducted, our meeting was productive. We decided we would have a membership drive to try and bring in money; we would set up workshops to be given by professionals; and we would put out a newsletter. As a first step, a meeting with professionals would be held to try and enlist their aid.

Several additional small meetings took place and literally hundreds of phone calls were made in the month of June. As a result many projects were soon put into effect.

Since money is a basic necessity for running any school, I personally undertook the mailing out of over a hundred and twenty-five letters to friends and relatives of mine and my parents, outside of Carlton. In the fundraising letter, I explained that a new school was being formed to help Shimmy and other youngsters with learning problems. I asked for their help. I felt some embarrassment at this, but reminded myself that the practice of charity is one of the mitzvos — commandments — that we, the Jewish people, adhere to. Our Sages teach us that our first responsibility is to give help to family and neighbors. And, I told myself, since my relatives give charity anyway, why should they not help someone they know? This was a worthy cause for their contribution.

PTACH's first contribution was made by a teacher in the girls' school: fifty dollars that her students had donated to charity over the course of the year. At their teacher's suggestion, the class had voted to give the money to PTACH.

With this fifty dollars plus the membership dues of the first twelve members, we paid for the stationery, the printing and the mailing of a thousand letters soliciting membership in PTACH.

A talented young woman, Tzippy, accepted the responsibility for putting out our first newsletter. She would gather and edit the articles, and seek advertisers to cover the cost of the printing.

Three women agreed to try to secure a booth for PTACH at the annual Jewish American Festival, a large gathering held in Carlton at the Inner Harbor on the Sunday and Monday of Labor Day weekend. Most of the Jewish schools, synagogues and organizations would participate in some way. Jewish art was exhibited and sold; kosher (and non-kosher) Jewish style foods were sold; and there were always various exhibits of a historical, educational and religious nature. The PTACH booth would give out literature — our newsletter — explaining the organization; what learning disabilities are; how children can be helped; and various suggestions. PTACH would also sell there, at a nominal price, a creative original package of games and educational materials that both teachers and parents could use.

A bake sale was planned for the summer.

Dr. Fields, a young Orthodox pediatrician and specialist in learning disabilities who had recently come to Carlton, agreed to give a lecture on the learning-disabled child, at the beginning of the next school year.

The first professional advisory board meeting took place in Hebrew Academy's Board Room. It was gratifying that thirteen of the professionals invited actually came. (I use the word "professionals" to mean those who were not the parents volunteering.) These professionals included two principals of special education schools in the public school sector, two special education teachers and a supervisor, a pediatrician, a social worker, a speech therapist, two optometrists, two psychologists, and the director of special education of the Bureau of Jewish Education.

For me — "just" a mother and an ordinary teacher — it seemed a formidable group at the time. I say "at the time" because besides becoming president of PTACH, over the years, through my close affiliation and involvement with special education, I have become something else: I consider myself a child advocate. Through all the years, I have learned many of the skills necessary for presenting to educational authorities the needs and legal rights of children with learning disabilities.

But back then, in June of 1979, I really wanted someone else to sit and chair that board meeting of formidable professionals. No one agreed to do it. And so, then and there, I adopted the advice of one of the ancient Sages of Israel, Hillel: "...where there are no men, strive to be a man" (*Pirkei Avos* 2:6). This motto has served as my prod ever since.

This has nothing to do with feminism. If there is a job that needs to be done, I make sure it gets done — this is how I can explain my perseverance. I wanted Shimmy to have a school; I believed such a school had to exist. Whatever was physically in my power to do — I was determined to do.

Although running a meeting may sound like a small challenge, at that time it was not. I presented our goals and accomplishments so far:

Our short-range goals were: (1) to start a self-contained class in Hebrew Academy in September for a preschool group of learning-disabled children; (2) to start a resource room in Hebrew Academy; and (3) to provide, if requested, part-time resource help to the other Jewish schools.

Our list of accomplishments included the following: (1) a questionnaire was mailed to the parent bodies of three day schools, to which twelve responses were received from the boys' schools; (2) two volunteer teachers visited Hebrew Academy and supplied the first-level screening; (3) a membership drive was begun; and (4) a newsletter was being prepared.

Various discussions ensued about what were the real special education needs in Carlton and how funding could be obtained. There was much lively discussion on all kinds of related subjects.

Mr. Stephen, a principal in the Carlton public school system, was pessimistic. "Where do you think you are going to get the funds to pay for your teachers? Have you worked out an exact budget? Do you know what your costs are? Are you going to be a separate, independent school, or part of Hebrew Academy?" And more.

I knew that I was the only one in a position to answer, yet I was not sure what to say. I took a deep breath and tried to project an image of self-confidence. "Well, we do not have an *exact* budget prepared, but we have begun collecting money to cover the teachers' salaries for September."

"What about the other nine months? How are you going to pay them the rest of the year?" he asked skeptically.

"We will raise the money. We have various fundraising ideas." I was getting defensive.

"Do you really intend to start the school year without knowing how you are going to pay your teachers? What will happen in January when you suddenly run out of money?" he persisted.

"I am determined that there will be a class in September, and I myself will take the responsibility to see that there will be enough money for the year," I answered, committing myself even further. "If we wait until we collect enough money, there will not be a school! I am convinced that people will give more readily to something that already exists, than to an idea."

Despite his initial skepticism, Mr. Stephen became involved. Ultimately two committees were established: the evaluation committee, whose purpose was to screen the children for eligibility for the program, and the education committee, whose function was to hire teachers and help develop program and curriculum. Mr. Stephen volunteered to chair the second committee and interview the three teaching candidates. It was his influence that succeeded in getting the board of Hebrew Academy to give us a classroom for PTACH's first kindergarten rent-free.

13

YEHOSHUA HAD TO report to his teaching job in the bungalow colony by July fourth at the latest, so I had to tie up loose ends quickly. As a matter of fact, I was very worried about leaving the city just when the momentum had been established. Would things fall apart without me pushing? I sat down and made an outline of all the projects for the summer, noting who was responsible for each task and who were the committee members. Everyone's phone numbers were included. Then I gave out copies of this list to Alice, Susanne and Shana, who promised to keep tabs on the summer activities and be in touch.

In turn, I promised to call them every week — in fact, I incurred a five-hundred-dollar phone bill that summer! I called the lawyer about drawing up incorporation papers. I called Tzippy to check on the progress of the newsletter. (At her suggestion, we decided to include in our first newsletter letters of endorsement from two prominent rabbis of our time. She contacted Rabbi Ruderman, the *Rosh Yeshiva* of the Rabbinical College in Baltimore, and I contacted a cousin who was studying in Rabbi Moshe Feinstein's yeshiva and who got for us a beautiful letter from "Reb Moishe" z"l.) Calls were made to check the progress of the booklet which we wanted to distribute at the Jewish American Festival; the new teachers were called, so we could discuss what materials had to be ordered and what they could make by themselves. Furniture for the classroom had to be found. And, of course, we looked for donations wherever possible.

I kept in constant touch with Alice because I was concerned about her following through with sending Barry to PTACH. She had a place for Barry in a public school with special education facilities, that she was reluctant to lose. I understood her concern, and in fact I myself had not yet informed Green Fields that Shimmy would not return in September — I was also keeping my options open, just in case. But I was definite about wanting Shimmy in a Jewish class, and I was confident that Miriam Bender, an articulate and competent young woman, would do an excellent job as his teacher.

Before I left Carlton for the summer, I had my first experience with "big-time" fundraising. One of the city's very wealthy businessmen was a well-known Jewish philanthropist who was known to have tremendous regard for Jewish education. Alice told me that he was a Holocaust survivor as well, and had suggested she and I approach him for a donation. "He may even give PTACH ten or twenty thousand dollars," she assured me, explaining that the rabbi of the synagogue where Mr. Rubel was a member had suggested to her that two of our mothers go and see him.

Upon hearing this exciting idea, I set up an appointment for Alice and me the very same evening. With a large donation like this, our classroom was assured! Then I would really relax for the summer (relax from PTACH, that is; this would give me time to "relax" with my children).

I picked up Alice and we drove to the Rubels' beautiful home in a wealthy suburb. Mr. and Mrs. Rubel themselves greeted us at the door. Alice and I were both nervous, and not sure how to begin. So I began with the simple truth. "Mr. and Mrs. Rubel," I said, "we are parents of little boys who have learning problems. Because of this, they cannot attend Hebrew Academy or *cheder*. But we want them to get a Jewish education, and so we are starting a special education school for Jewish children. Mr. Mendelson, who goes to your synagogue, and who is the supervisor of special education for Carlton city, serves on our professional advisory board."

"Oh, Mr. Mendelson! Yes, he is a very fine man," commented Mrs. Rubel. I felt encouraged and continued.

"We hope to open with a full-day class for four, as well as a resource program for those children who can, for most of the day, remain in their regular class, but need help in specific areas." I was trying to sound knowledgeable and "professional."

A phone call interrupted my speech. When Mr. Rubel returned, Alice resumed the appeal.

"It is so important for Jewish children to be in a Jewish environment. Otherwise, they will lose their identity, and we have lost so many Jews already in this generation."

"What do you want from us?" Mrs. Rubel asked pragmatically, cutting short Alice's speech.

I replied. "We were hoping that you would be able to help us with a donation. We have many volunteers, but we have to pay the teachers. So..." I was not sure how to continue.

"We are already committed to the girls' school and to Hebrew Academy, as well as to the Jewish Federation and our synagogue," Mr. Rubel told me, "and we cannot overextend ourselves." My heart sank. "However, we will give you something now and in December you can ask for the same."

He then wrote a check for $250. Alice and I thanked him profusely and left. Two hundred and fifty dollars was the largest single donation PTACH had yet received, but instead of being overjoyed, we felt let down. We had both expected a donation of thousands of dollars. After that experience, I learned to be cautious with my expectations, and I hesitated before accepting the expectations of others.

14

THE EIGHT WEEKS that we spent in the bungalow colony did not bring me a respite from my fundraising activities. On the contrary! This colony had doubled in population from the first time we were there, and I decided to take advantage of the opportunity to approach over a hundred Jewish families. Every day I would spend an hour going from door to door asking for help for PTACH of Carlton. I would set out in the mornings, taking baby Yona in the carriage, while the older three were in day camp. (That year Shimmy went like a veteran.)

Though it was awkward for me at first, it became a very fulfilling experience in many ways. I collected over $1,000, and I also met people who themselves had children with difficulties, or who had friends and relatives whose children had various problems. These people were interested in talking to me and learning more about the subject. One mother had a two-and-a-half-year-old who was not yet walking. She asked me what she should do. I was amazed that she had not begun investigating the problem sooner. I am no longer amazed. I have seen that parents will often deny to themselves for as long as they can that a problem exists. It is natural to keep hoping that with time the child will outgrow the problem and catch up. It is very difficult to acknowledge that one's child is not entirely "normal" or perfect.

One particularly exciting fundraising experience I had that summer was when I went to the Satmar Rebbetzin for a donation. The Satmar are a Chassidic sect who are ultra-Orthodox. The Satmar Rebbe was considered one of the greatest and most knowledgeable Rabbis in the world, and his wife, the Rebbetzin, was known to be very charitable.

Since I do not know how to speak much Yiddish, which remained the language of these European chassidim even in America, my friend Chana Leah agreed to come along and be my translator. We dressed up in our Shabbos clothes, for the Rebbe and Rebbetzin are accorded the respect one would give to a king and queen. Although we always dressed modestly, now we dressed as the Satmar women dressed. In order not to appear offensive, we both wore dark stockings and tied scarves on over our wigs.

As we set out, we felt a little funny dressed in our Sabbath finery with our double head-coverings on an ordinary hot summer day in the middle of the week.

The Rebbe's summer home was a ten-minute ride away. We found the house easily: a stately white building with a short driveway off the road. In front of the property tall evergreen trees lined the road, affording the Rebbe and his household some privacy.

We parked the car on the side of the road and began to walk up the driveway. Suddenly, a man and two women emerged from the house. One woman was around sixty, heavyset, and wore a brown scarf over a simple brown wig. The other woman was much younger. She had a beautiful face, and wore no makeup. She was neat and very modestly attired, with a black scarf stylishly knotted at the side of her head, a long skirt, and thick black stockings.

Chana Leah urged me on. Addressing the older woman, she began to speak in Yiddish. "We are coming on behalf of a school for Jewish children with learning problems. They cannot go to regular *cheder* because of their problems."

The older woman interrupted her, saying that the Rebbetzin was just leaving and was in a hurry. Chana Leah and I looked at each other in surprise. The younger woman was the Rebbetzin!

I turned to her and began with the few Yiddish words I knew: "*Ich bin a mamma* of a *yingel* with these problems, and I want to help him get a Jewish education."

The Rebbetzin turned to the man and said something in Yiddish to him. He reached into his pocket and gave her something, which she then handed to me: a $100 bill! She looked directly at me and wished me "*Hatzlachah*" — success. Since they were obviously in a hurry we quickly left, but first we thanked the Rebbetzin profusely. Chana Leah firmly believed that my four words in Yiddish — *Ich bin a mamma* (I am a mother) — were the words that made the hurrying Rebbetzin pause. Her compassionate heart could not allow a mother's plea to go unanswered.

At the end of July, we returned to Carlton for a few days. Because of his increased responsibilities in the high school, Yehoshua had to touch base there, and I was happy to have the opportunity to check on the progress of my projects, first hand. While I was there, a professional advisory board meeting was held and Alice and I were pleased with the attendance of a few new professionals. Interest in PTACH was spreading. The bake sale held in front of a large supermarket had brought in $210. Membership responses were continuing to come in.

The pamphlet of games that Shana was assembling was made up of contributions from several teachers and therapists. The pamphlet contained suggestions of various activities and games for parents to play with their children. One example, presented by Miriam Bender, demonstrated how standard playing cards can improve children's number concepts: the game of *War* increases a child's awareness of "greater than" and "less than" (the ten of diamonds is greater than the four of clubs).

That visit brought me the wonderful news that Hebrew Academy had formally consented to our starting a resource program in addition to the self-contained classroom in their school.

One serious problem that I confronted in those few days was Alice's decision to send Barry for only half a day. Since we were still an experimental first-year program, she could not bring herself to risk losing Barry's place in the public school. I was upset, since this meant that Shimmy would not be able to learn for a whole day in this environment we were creating — for there were only the two boys so far: Barry and Shimmy. Yehoshua rationalized that fortunately we still had placement for Shimmy in the afternoons, and in Green Fields they would give him speech therapy weekly. We were lucky we would have even half a day of a Jewish special education class, he assured me.

As disappointed as I was, I told myself, "*Gam zo l'tovah* — this too is for the best." This is a principle which Orthodox Jews rely on, for we cannot comprehend many things that have happened to us collectively or individually. Who can perceive anything good about a misfortune when it occurs? Looking back, however, we often discern the good which results from a seemingly bad occurrence.

PTACH was to begin on a small scale. We had a master teacher and an assistant teacher in the half-day self-contained class. We also had a resource teacher for fifteen hours a week to work with five boys in Hebrew Academy. Our total budget, including salaries, educational materials and operating expenses, came to less than $24,000 for the first year.

I had resigned from my job as a teacher in the girls' school and intended to devote the entire year to involvement in all aspects of PTACH. Most of the time would be spent in fundraising, a new venture for me. That first year we made enough money to cover our budget each month — just barely. One month I even personally borrowed $200 from a friend, so that our teachers would be paid on time. The responsibility became mine. I could manage $24,000, but I don't know if I could have managed more!

Alice was still annoyed that PTACH would be housed in Hebrew Academy. She and another parent formed a kind of alliance and tried to push their opinions to the front.

Mr. and Mrs. Mandel had a son of Shimmy's age, who was in the same special educational program as Alice's son Barry. I tried very hard to convince them to send their son to PTACH.

"We do not want to experiment with our child," Mrs. Mandel answered firmly. "Children's Educational Center has a good kindergarten and Ezra has been making nice progress there. If your PTACH really gets off the ground, we will consider enrolling Ezra then."

We returned to the bungalow colony for the last three weeks, and I tried to relax. My two sisters were both there with their children for that part of the summer, and all the cousins enjoyed each other's company.

Labor Day weekend brought the Jewish American Festival in Carlton. Although the PTACH booth was small and almost hidden away in a little corner, it got mention in the local newspaper as one of the few really educational exhibits. We did not make much money selling our booklets, but we did get some positive publicity. In fact, we were becoming aware that public relations was a whole area that needed to be dealt with. We were fortunate that at the time, September 1979, the Carlton Jewish Weekly was doing a feature on special educa- tion. Someone suggested that the reporter interview me about PTACH.

I found it exciting to think that my work was so important that someone would actually interview me, and I recognized the opportunity to gain support for PTACH. As I became more and more involved in promoting, developing and expanding PTACH, I ceased to view interviews or pictures in the paper as a sign of personal accomplishment: PTACH was the essential thing. But there was a negative side to the increasing responsibility and obligation I took upon myself. Internal politics and power struggles created increasingly uncomfortable feelings.

One day I looked so glum that my sister, who met me in school, said, "Rivka, you are going to have to decide if you really can handle this involvement in PTACH. You know, anyone in the public eye gets a lot of criticism. If you cannot take it and you let it depress you, then forget it; it's not for you. You have a family to take care of and they don't deserve a depressed mother and wife. Maybe you should just let someone else be president."

"But who would do it?" I asked.

"I don't know, but if you are going to take every little thing to heart, then *you* shouldn't be doing it."

Yehoshua tried to encourage me with words of wisdom. His Rebbe, Rabbi Weinberg, had taught him once in the name of Rabbi Ruderman z"l, the following: "It is written in the Torah: 'Love your fellowman as yourself.' About one's brother, it is written: 'Do not hate your brother.' The Bible knows that sibling rivalry can kill the love one feels for his brother, so realistically we are told: If you cannot love him, at least do not hate him!

"Now, when it comes to a king, or a president, we are told: 'A president in your nation do not curse.' Since we are never commanded anything unreasonable, it is presumably natural to hate our leaders."

This little "sermon" on the wisdom of the Bible served as a great source of help and encouragement to me, both at that time and during other times of conflict within the organizational aspect of PTACH.

15

PTACH STARTED FUNCTIONING as a school two days after Labor Day in September 1979. Only two little five-year-olds attended the self-contained class the first month: Shimmy and Barry. Shimmy was very pleased to be able to walk to school by himself — his classroom was located on the ground floor of the Hebrew Academy high school building. Alice was relieved that the classroom was a little removed from the elementary school. I was absolutely thrilled that my son was attending a Jewish special educational school.

Every day at noon the county school bus would honk its horn in front of the high school building, and Shimmy would happily wave goodbye to his teachers, *Morah* Miriam and *Morah* Amy. Then he'd be on his way to Green Fields. Alice would come at the same time and transport Barry to his afternoon school. (They lived in the city district and Barry went to a public school not far from his house.)

School had started right before the High Holidays, the holiest days in the Jewish year. Therefore, the classroom had been decorated by the teachers with lovely pictures relating to the Holidays. Rosh Hashanah, the Jewish New Year, is symbolized by three themes: *Teshuvah* — Repentance, *Tefillah* — Prayer, and *Tzedakah* — Charity. On one wall were pictures illustrating these basic ideas: a shofar, which is blown to awaken the Jewish people to repentance; a prayer book; and a charity box with a slot for coins (a familiar item to a child from a Jewish home). For Yom Kippur, a picture of a balancing scale was hung up: Our sins and our merits are judged on that day. These pictures were so familiar to me, that I took it for granted that their significance would be clear to Shimmy as well. But the fact is that Shimmy needed to be taught those three well-known words — "*Teshuvah, Tefillah, Tzedakah*" — over and over, until he could pronounce them and remember them. These basic concepts had to be explained and reinforced until he could understand. That is exactly what Jewish special education is about. While teaching these basic Jewish concepts, the teachers worked on developing other skills. The boys worked at cutting out the curved shape of the ram's horn, a skill all kindergarten teachers try to teach their students. Cutting helps build up fine motor muscles.

The children also pasted and colored and matched pictures, all common enough activities for a kindergarten, but what was different was both the content and the pace. In PTACH, the teacher would reinforce their knowledge of colors and numbers, teaching rote counting and then conceptualization of the numbers. The pictures that were used included religious objects: one Torah, two Sabbath candles, three prayer books, four wine cups.

Although I was not teaching, I was always on the run. Little Yona came along with me in the car when I went about my errands — in addition to being a busy housewife and mother, I was busy setting up parlor meetings for fundraising, and a workshop for the purpose of educating the public.

Shimmy was settled and happy; Yosef and Chaya were busy in their classes. Whenever possible, I would take the children along with me to my various fundraising affairs. These were exciting excursions for them, and they especially loved going to bake sales, where they would always sample cupcakes, some cookies, or whatever there was. It was not until mid-October that I once again realized that things were not totally ideal for Shimmy.

I received a note from Mrs. Brown, Shimmy's new teacher in Green Fields, inviting me to go over Shimmy's Individual Education Plan (IEP) with her. (Each child in a special education class has written up for him personal long term and short term goals with specific methods designated to achieve them.) As I entered his classroom, I was struck by the contrast of the decorations in this class with those in his morning class. Here were no rams' horns or charity boxes, no apples and honey; I was overwhelmed by bright round orange pumpkins, and witches on broomsticks, marking the approaching Halloween.

The discussion began with the teacher expressing her disapproval of Shimmy's attending a different program in the morning. She felt that we should send Shimmy to Green Fields all day where he would benefit from constant involvement, from morning until 3 P.M. "Now, he comes in late," she said, "and he misses so much."

I explained to her that since religious practice was an integral part of our life as Orthodox Jews, it was important to us that Shimmy get his religious training in a professional school program, like all our other children were doing.

"This is the 'least restrictive environment' for him," I said, using my professional jargon, but then added spontaneously and not so diplomatically, "I wish PTACH were a whole-day program — he would benefit greatly."

Mrs. Brown appeared not too pleased with that comment. I could sense that we would not share the same rapport that Ms. Baxter and I had. To make matters worse, I did not like the IEP at all. "I think you are setting very low goals for Shimmy," I told her. "In my opinion, he has surpassed them already. He can identify red, yellow, blue and green; he can count by rote until five — at least; I think you are simply underestimating his capacity. I am not sure I want to agree to this IEP. I have to think about it."

I left the meeting very annoyed, and called Shimmy's PTACH teacher right away. Miriam promised to schedule a meeting with Mrs. Brown, in the hope that the morning and afternoon programs would be coordinated.

Two days later I got a note from Mrs. Brown asking me to send a costume for Shimmy for the Halloween party. To me, that was more evidence of her lack of understanding. I kept Shimmy home the day of the party; none of the treats were kosher, and I did not want him celebrating Halloween in any way. Since it is a pagan custom in origin, we consider it inappropriate for Orthodox Jewish children to participate in Halloween festivities.

Shortly afterwards, Miriam met with me after spending a couple of hours with Mrs. Brown. Miriam's recommendation was that I just relax and let things ride in Green Fields. There, she reminded me, Shimmy was getting speech therapy once a week, and this was very important for him. PTACH could not provide even that much. Also, she added, since Mrs. Brown was expecting a baby and would be leaving, there would be a replacement who may prove to be better. "So, Rivka, my advice is to let Shimmy continue in Green Fields for half a day. And you might as well agree to the IEP," Miriam told me. "The structured environment, and the constant reinforcement of the skills he has learned, can only be good for him. Mrs. Brown claims that Shimmy is not consistently able to identify the colors, even though I know that in the morning he can. Who knows, maybe soon he will show her that he can. Anyway, I suggest you try not to show Mrs. Brown your displeasure — she seems a bit insulted by your attitude."

I appreciated Miriam's advice. I agreed to the IEP, signed it and sent it back to school with Shimmy. Nonetheless, I became more determined to see that next year Shimmy would have a full-day program with PTACH.

16

THE YEAR WAS characterized by fundraising activities, organizational meetings and turmoil. There was not enough structure in the PTACH organization itself. Since the school program had been started by parents, some of the parents felt they could dominate all aspects of the actual educational methodology.

A third child, Allan Denberg, entered Shimmy's class, which was wonderful for Shimmy — another potential friend. However, the Denbergs, both intelligent and educated, proved to be very tough people to work with. Allan's father felt that he knew enough to tell the teachers what method they should use when teaching his son. Although Miriam felt that a different reading series might be more effective, Mr. Denberg insisted on the linguistic approach. Three months later he admitted that it was not the approach he had intended — he had simply mixed up the terminology.

Internal politics was a source of great stress. One of the mothers expressed concern over my "power" and even questioned whether all the children were getting the help they needed, suggesting that my son was the prime beneficiary of the program.

This was, of course, ridiculous. There were two teachers who gave individual attention to each of the three boys, who were all progressing at their own rates. All three were learning.

Barry was the brightest of the three. He had behavioral problems, but academically he showed much potential. It was difficult for me to understand Alice. I was so happy to see Barry's progress and only hoped Shimmy would do as well soon. It seemed that Alice was having a hard time adjusting to a successful Barry. She was used to a child with learning problems.

These were the problems we were immersed in through the fall and winter.

The holiday of Purim was approaching, and the PTACH teachers were preparing the children for the holiday. Each child had colored his own pictorial scroll of Esther. I was so proud when Shimmy brought his home, and was amazed at how well he was able to tell the story of Purim with the help of the attractive pictures. He still refused to wear a costume like the other children. It was not something in his usual routine. And he would not go out to deliver the baskets of cake and fruit to our neighbors, even refusing to go in the car with Yehoshua to deliver the *shalach manos* to friends who lived farther away. He couldn't easily handle new experiences.

Yosef and Chaya had a wonderful time dressing up as a little Mordechai and Queen Esther. For every *shalach manos* they delivered, the recipient would reward them either with Purim money or a special treat. Little Yona wore the clown's costume again. Shimmy knew it was Purim. He was not frightened. He just was not ready to get involved himself. Nonetheless, we were very pleased to see the improvement over last year.

Over the years I have continued to measure growth in Shimmy by his behavior on Purim. We have noted changes in Shimmy's behavior and comprehension of all the many Jewish holidays, and we have seen progress each year. But that terrible Purim when Shimmy was four-and-a-half and could not relate at all to his surroundings remains etched in my memory. That Purim forced me to realize that Shimmy was different.

My dream was fulfilled and the following year PTACH's full-day program came into being. Both Barry and Allan had left but two new boys Shimmy's age had joined the class. They were all able to join the regular first grade in Hebrew Academy for prayers in the morning — although Shimmy still could not read Hebrew well. He knew the blessings and chants by heart and he loved them. I was thrilled that he fit in well with the regular first grade for the first fifteen minutes of the morning. Then he would return to the self-contained class and get instruction on his level. During recess time, the three boys would once again join the first grade, and in the afternoon, their special curriculum would include reading in English as well as math skills.

With the approach of his seventh birthday, Shimmy was reevaluated by a psychologist from the Carlton county public school system. By this time I had learned to demand what I felt was necessary. I requested that the psychologist who would be testing him not be the one who had previously seen him.

Dr. Benchley, a friendly, smiling woman in her thirties, met with me before meeting with Shimmy. To prepare myself, I had read and acquainted myself with information about various means used for testing intelligence. I was under the impression that the Wechsler test would suit him more than the Stanford-Binet, since the Stanford-Binet test is geared for children with good auditory skills. Because Shimmy's speech was his weakest point, I felt he would perform better with the Wechsler test. This also tests cognitive skills but employs more of the visual skills in testing.

Dr. Benchley treated me with kindness and respect, listening to my point of view with interest. That meeting with her was one of my best experiences with a professional dealing with my child. Although I believe I spoke intelligently, I am certain that even if I had not done so, she would have listened politely and seriously.

Shimmy was tested during two sessions. He was friendly and tried to please. Dr. Benchley met with me to give me the results. (Yehoshua was not able to come, as he still taught in the mornings and was the assistant principal in charge of the Hebrew Academy high school.)

"Mrs. Walburg, I am sure you will be pleased with the results of Shimmy's tests," Dr. Benchley began. "I administered the Wechsler as you requested. Shimmy's strengths were clearly in visual memory, matching and discriminating. His average score was 79-80 which places him in the low-normal range," she said. "At the same time, I gave him an abridged version of the Stanford-Binet test, and in this test too he showed improvement and scored in the high 70's."

"Oh, how wonderful — I am so happy!" I burst out. I was beaming. "I *never* could really bring myself to believe that Shimmy was *re...retarded!*"

Dr. Benchley explained to me that there is a whole spectrum that measures intelligence. Finding the right label is not the crucial reason for testing children; rather, tests are helpful in showing a child's areas of strength and of weakness. "And," she emphasized, "IQ scores can improve if a child is given appropriate stimulation and education in those areas."

I left the meeting filled with tremendous hope and renewed determination to see that more children would benefit from PTACH. I wanted our program to accommodate every child who applied. I wanted every parent of a Jewish child with a problem to come forward and try to get help.

With Tzippy and Susanne's help, I put out three to four newsletters a year. These were sent to the parents of all children attending Jewish schools, and to other names on

PTACH's growing mailing list. We held workshops open to the public several times a year. They were usually enthusiastically received, but by a small group. Slowly, but steadily, new members of the Carlton community were becoming interested.

One man, Ed Raynor, suggested that we hold a dinner. A banquet would be a good fundraiser, he pointed out, as well as a means of publicizing our programs. Though now a successful businessman, he told us that he himself probably would have benefited from some help when he was a student. Ed enlisted the aid of some of his friends. And the PTACH organization grew. Yaakov Davidowitz (a talented Rebbe and Hebrew teacher in Hebrew Academy), Mrs. Brunner (an amateur photographer), Tzippy (the editor of our newsletter) and I got together to produce a slide show explaining PTACH. A professional television announcer volunteered to narrate the script. Yaakov was the technical director. He synchronized the slides with the narration and appropriate background music.

When the lights went on after the slide show there were few dry eyes. The frustration of the learning-disabled child was depicted graphically — but the major theme was one of hope.

17

I GAVE BIRTH to Yaakov, our fifth child, in the summer of 1982. Shimmy adjusted well to his new brother. Yona did not. Yona became a behavioral problem, and this initiated another difficult period in our lives in which we had to acknowledge that not one, but two of our children had problems. Ultimately Yona was diagnosed as hyperactive. The doctors attributed this to the stress he experienced in his premature and difficult birth.

So totally overwhelming and engrossing were Shimmy's problems, their diagnosis, and my coming to terms with them, that it never occurred to me that Yona had a problem as well. The main thing that had concerned me was that he did not exhibit any of Shimmy's problems, and I was relieved when he spoke early and showed good cognitive skills. I felt that if he was not like Shimmy then he was all right!

As an infant, Yona constantly suffered from colds and earaches, to which I attributed his equally constant irritability. Looking back, I see that I was all-too-willing to ignore signs of trouble. But Yaakov's birth highlighted them. Yona's behavior could not be ignored. For the months that followed, I left Shimmy to the expert care of his competent teachers and I devoted myself to caring for little Yaakov and dealing with Yona's problem.

It ultimately took over a year of perseverance, taking him to doctors, therapists, and various professionals, to determine what his difficulties were and what could be done to help him. I was determined, and successful, in getting him accepted into a government program.

Initially, the county school system was prepared to recommend Yona's placement in a special education nursery. But I was certain that this was not what Yona needed, and I fought to have him tested and retested. When ultimately I was awarded his right to occupational therapy through the public school system, I felt I had won a victory. All along I had encountered hostile professionals who did not want to help children from private schools.

Legally, any handicapped child is entitled to speech, physical or occupational therapy — no matter what school he attends. In reality, however, those children in public schools are most likely to receive this help simply because children from private schools cannot be easily referred by their homeroom teacher. There is much red tape and complicated arrangements that need to be made, including transportation, in order to ensure that the private school child receives the service in the public school in his home district.

Now, when I look back at my years in Carlton, it seems I was living the life of a juggler. Our baby Yaakov needed care. Yona's needs took time to be met. Shimmy was "in the air" at the time (his teachers and school program were dealing with him at the time — not I). Thank God, Yosef and Chaya were doing well in their respective schools. But I was still managing a home and family of small children, and running an organization. Once Yona was placed to my satisfaction, and a major fundraising activity for PTACH was completed, I was "free" to devote time to Shimmy again.

After his eye operation, Shimmy had continued to squint. I took him for checkups every six months, and although his vision remained good in each eye, he still did not use his eyes together on a regular basis. Dr. Levy, an ophthalmologist in Carlton, offered me the prognosis very calmly: "Eventually Shimmy may lose sight in one eye." I was dumbfounded. He continued, "As time goes by he will begin to favor one eye, and ultimately the other eye will cease to function due to lack of exercise."

"Are you saying that he will go blind in one eye? That's terrible!" I exclaimed.

"I am saying that it is a possiblity — but it is not so terrible, Mrs. Walburg. Believe me, people can function very well with the use of only one eye." As Dr. Levy was speaking, I noticed that he had a peculiarly intense stare. I felt defensive, suddenly, and it occurred to me that perhaps the doctor was blind in one eye. Maybe I was imagining it, but I did not say anything further.

Not long after this examination, I met Jean, a newcomer to Carlton. Jean had attended one of PTACH's workshops, in which a social worker had given a talk about parents' reactions to discovering they have a problem child. She described the emotions that a bereaved person experiences and claimed that parents of handicapped children go through a similar experience. Denial, anger, guilt, mourning and recovery were discussed. The emphasis was on recovery. Jean asked interesting questions and seemed very intelligent. She, thank God, had no handicapped children but came to the meeting simply because she wanted to get involved as a volunteer fundraiser. She wanted to learn more about PTACH.

I spoke to Jean after the meeting and learned that her father-in-law was an optometrist in Chicago. His specialty was visual therapy, something I had never heard of before.

Visual therapy is a relatively new field, in which optometrists specially trained in visual problems provide various exercises for the patient, the purpose of which is to improve the ability to see. Shimmy's problem was inconsistent binocular vision — the use of his two eyes together — and weak eye-hand coordination. I knew that Shimmy had very poor depth perception because he used one eye at a time, most of the time. This knowledge helped explain his slowness in learning to walk up and down stairs, and his fear of going down the hill behind our house.

Dr. and Mrs. Stern, Jean's in-laws, were coming to visit the following week, she told me, and she suggested I meet with her father-in-law and see if he could offer some suggestions for Shimmy.

Not only was he happy to see me, but Dr. Stern was kind enough to informally examine Shimmy, Yona and Yaakov. He was pleased to report that Yaakov's eyes were fine, but Yona, like Shimmy, had strabismus. This was not a complete surprise to me. Dr. Stern directed us to the practice of Dr. Hudson in Oceanview. Dr. Hudson and his associates were specialists in visual training.

Shimmy became a patient, and twice a week either Yehoshua or I would drive to Oceanview to take Shimmy for a forty-five minute session of visual therapy. We tried taking Yona also for visual therapy but he was very uncooperative and unruly. Dr. Hudson recommended that we wait awhile with Yona and concentrate first on Shimmy.

To our relief we found that our Blue Cross-Blue Shield policy covered 80% of the cost of the therapy, but the remaining 20% was still expensive. We went twice a week, and the trip itself cost money. Altogether, visual therapy was a financially demanding proposition for us. I was somewhat relieved to have to pay only for Shimmy.

I mention this to introduce the problem of financial dilemma that many parents of handicapped children face. Using myself as an example, on the one hand, I want to do whatever I can to help my children improve. I honestly believe it's cost-effective to give intensive treatment to children when they are young. With early constant help, a learning-handicapped child has a good chance of reaching his appropriate level quickly and avoiding the development of emotional problems.

On the other hand, however, there is almost no end to what a parent can spend. I am constantly forced to make choices and decisions. For me, the deciding factor has always been: what can I not do without. I intentionally put this in the negative, for there are many things from which Shimmy could benefit. In addition to the well-known physical, occupational, speech, and psychological therapies, there are also other areas of therapy including visual, music, and art; there are water skills, equestrian skills, gymnastics, etc. I once read that horseback riding effected an amazing improvement in a child with Down's Syndrome. This became evident in his motor skills, his posture, his concentration powers and most of all, in his self-assurance. It sounded so tempting, yet could we possibly afford to put Shimmy in such a program?

Shimmy could not do without a Jewish education: I know that his identity as a member of his society is the most crucial element in his feeling of self-worth. Ostensibly, we had the choice of putting him into a public school special education program that would be free. But for Shimmy, our little Jewish boy, this was not an option.

When Shimmy had trouble communicating, he became physically aggressive and began to overeat. Speech therapy was a priority at that time.

I did not agree with Dr. Levy that losing vision in one eye was not such a bad prospect. It is true that people can function and live normal lives with sight in only one eye, but why should we just allow Shimmy to get another disability? Visual therapy seemed to be a possible way of combating this problem. For him it was crucial. Yet for Yona, I was not sure that visual therapy was crucial — at that time. I worried about the financial strain of having two children in visual therapy. It was a relief that the doctor said to wait.

18

AFTER TWO-AND-A-HALF YEARS of visual therapy, I tried to secure an occupational therapy program for Shimmy. He was definitely benefiting from the therapy. His eye-hand coordination had improved. Once again I encountered strong opposition from various professionals from the Carlton county public school system.

Shimmy was nine at the time, and enrolled in a private elementary school. I had to first send a written request to the public school in my district. The principal then forwarded the request to the department of evaluation from Carlton county. I let them know that I would like to exercise my legal right and be present at the team meeting, along with the private school teachers, when it was to be decided if Shimmy was eligible to receive occupational therapy.

At the meeting, I sensed much hostility on the part of yet another psychologist from Carlton county. She had never met Shimmy, and I could not understand why she seemed so negative towards me at that first meeting. (After my aggressive behavior at the meeting, she became even more negative!) The meeting was chaired by Mr. Karls, principal of the Crown Avenue elementary school. His assistant principal was present, as was a speech therapist, occupational therapist, psychologist, special education therapist from Carlton county, the school nurse, and Miss David, a teacher from PTACH. At least I had one person definitely on my side.

Shimmy was one of several children being reviewed. Miss David and I were asked to wait while the rest of the team had a chance to quickly review his records. When we finally entered the office, which was crowded with all the unfamiliar personnel, I found I was quite tense.

"We have reviewed your request and would like to hear in your own words what exactly you would like for Shimmy. I note here," said Mr. Karls, "that a place had been provided for Shimmy in Green Fields and subsequently in Harrow Road but you chose not to put Shimmy in these special classes."

"That is correct," I answered quickly. Altogether I found I was speaking very quickly. "We are Orthodox Jews and we felt the best and least restrictive environment for Shimmy would be in PTACH, a special education program which provides the particular help that my son needs, teaching him basic skills in an environment that is compatible with his religious upbringing. In addition to reading and math, he also receives instruction by qualified certified special education teachers in religious subjects. My husband and I felt it was very important that Shimmy receive an education, on his level, that is comparable to the Jewish education his siblings are receiving. This is important for his being able to fit into our society."

"And so why are you turning to the public school system now?" demanded the psychologist.

"PTACH is an effective non-profit school but it is new and small and poor. Being involved in the fundraising for it, I know that there are no funds for an occupational therapist. Since it is the legal right of every handicapped child to receive the help he needs from the government, I am requesting that Shimmy receive occupational therapy. The reality is that for two years we have been paying for him to have visual therapy. The cost has become prohibitive. Our insurance no longer covers it. Occupational therapy with an emphasis on sensory perception offers many of the same exercises that he has been receiving. His visual and motor problems would benefit greatly from occupational therapy."

"Well, Mrs. Walburg, had Shimmy been in a special education program from the county, I am certain that if his teachers had felt he needed this help he would have received it. But since you put him a private school..."

"What's the difference!" I angrily interrupted the psychologist. "Private-school children are entitled, according to the law, to receive help."

Not everyone was hostile. The assistant principal intervened. "Mrs. Walburg, you are right that any handicapped child should be able to receive the therapy he needs. The procedure that needs to be followed is the following: Shimmy should be evaluated by an occupational therapist, and then we will meet again to decide how we can help your son."

The meeting was over. The nurse smiled kindly and said, "I will call you to inform you when Shimon's evaluation will take place."

I left the building feeling somewhat shaky. I was sure I had stated the facts and my opinions clearly, but I felt that I had been in a battle and that one of my enemies was anti-Semitism. I would never say that aloud. It was possible that public school professionals are sensitive about children leaving the public school system; perhaps any private school child would have met with the same reaction. Perhaps I was being paranoid — but those were the vibrations I had gotten at the meeting.

Miss Feeny evaluated Shimmy during two forty-five-minute sessions. Despite her petite size and her cute Orphan Annie curls, she turned out to be very firm and capable in dealing with children with short attention spans. Shimmy was cooperative and when ultimately he did become Miss Feeny's pupil, she enjoyed his eagerness to work. When, upon later reevaluation, Shimmy measured a very small degree of improvement, Miss Feeny was surprised with the test results and concluded that while Shimmy had improved, he simply does not respond well in a testing environment.

Yona had progressed very rapidly in the two years Miss Feeny had worked with him. With Shimmy it was a very slow process — but steadily he did show improvement.

19

THE FIRST TWO years of the establishment of PTACH were years of totally time-consuming involvement. Over the course of the next three years I was probably involved in just as many fundraising projects, but nonetheless my life slowly began to expand and include other things. This is Shimmy's story, but he was the cause and effect of many things.

For one thing, I became a "hot line" for Jewish parents of handicapped children. Though most of the callers were from Carlton, over the years I have received calls from as far away as California and Texas, as well as from Detroit, Cleveland, Atlanta, Boston, Chicago, Birmingham, Philadelphia, Montreal and the New York area.

Some calls were from parents or teachers who wanted to know how they could start a PTACH program in their city. Sometimes I could not really help in any way other than to provide a sympathetic ear; at other times I was gratified to be able to offer concrete assistance and direct parents to their local child-find center, which would help them secure services for their child.

I also advised parents of their legal rights, and encouraged them to fight to obtain whatever therapy was needed. I had the privilege of meeting many parents and sharing their stories, and I grew rich knowing these people. For every despairing parent I encountered, I met another with great fortitude. I learned how to be more sensitive and more appreciative.

One local call came from a parent of a hearing-impaired child who was approaching Bar Mitzvah — age thirteen. Mrs. Bern wanted her son Harry to be called up to the Torah for a blessing. He was attending a public school for the hearing-impaired and had received almost no Jewish education.

"We are not strictly observant Jews," she told me, "but we do want our son to 'have' a Bar Mitzvah. Does PTACH have a program to teach him?" Mrs. Bern asked.

"No," I replied, "but I know that a branch of the Associated Jewish Charities, the Carlton Jewish Education Council, has afternoon programs for public-school children. Among their Sunday school afternoon classes are special classes for handicapped children — try contacting their office."

Mrs. Bern was happy and grateful for the information. I hung up the phone, suddenly amazed. The previous year I would not have been able to help her at all. I had acquired much useful information but there were still so many people who did not know how to get help.

When I went for my four-week checkup after Yaakov's birth, I met a young woman in the doctor's office who said, "Hello, aren't you Rivka Walburg from PTACH?"

"Yes," I answered, a little surprised. "And what is your name?" I asked.

"Zena Eagel. I just had a baby too. He has Down's Syndrome." I hesitated a moment as the words *Down's Syndrome* flashed through my head. Then I quickly said, "*Mazal tov! Mazal tov!*"

"Thank you," she said, grateful at my congratulations. I recognized her thanks as being true appreciation. She had wanted me to acknowledge the joy in the birth of her new child. He may not be perfect, but he was her baby, and a new little soul whose life should be valued.

I thank God my hesitation was so brief, and regret I hesitated at all. Yet this encounter had a profound influence on me. I went to the library and took out a book on Down's Syndrome, for I suddenly wanted to understand more about it. One thing I learned was that the phrase Zena had used, Down's Syndrome, is the correct term for this condition which is caused by a chromosomal abnormality. ("Mongoloid" is considered a negative, derogatory label. Children with Down's Syndrome have, among other unique physical characteristics, flattish noses and eyes with an oriental cast. Their features resemble "Mongolian" features, and from this the term originated.)

Zena Eagel and her husband, determined to help their son achieve his potential, enrolled him in special programs from infancy. We kept in touch for a few years, happy to share the achievements of our sons.

Nita Rabinowitz gave birth to a little boy with a severe hearing loss. She did not classify her son Yitzy as deaf, but rather as hearing-impaired. (The word "deaf" is not an acceptable term, unless one means totally deaf.) Nita became something of a recluse during the first year of her son's life. She did not socialize, but rather took the baby every day to a program which worked on teaching hearing-impaired babies to hear. Hearing aids amplified any possible sound they were capable of detecting. Nita herself learned how to talk and enunciate to Yitzy so that he would learn to hear as much as possible and to read lips.

Nita and I sometimes met each other at the supermarket. I would smile and greet her each time, and as the years went by we became friends. Yitzy began to talk — not perfectly clearly — but with evidence of much intelligence. A very cute little boy, he was also bright and had many friends. In addition to the children on his block with whom he played happily, he also met many others. Nita did not remain a recluse for long. She took Yitzy for swimming lessons, and to an arts and crafts class. She provided him with the opportunity to socialize with other children his age in various environments, and as a result Yitzy seldom suffered the loneliness and isolation that children who cannot hear often experience.

When Cindy Dane, an artist in Carlton, gave birth to a little girl who was born with no optic nerve, people were shocked and saddened. A talented person for whom vision is life, whose eyes are part of her tools, Cindy was able to face this misfortune as a challenge. Her daughter could not see, but she could walk and hear and develop. At a parent support-group meeting, Cindy requested that the theme of the subsequent meeting be: "What are the good things that have come with my child's having a handicap." The suggestion alone evoked many positive responses. All the mothers had to go home and find something good to share next time.

At the next meeting, Cindy told us, "I value so many aspects of life now, things that I used to take for granted. What a blessing it is to be able to walk and talk and think. I try to instill in all my children how grateful we should be to the Almighty for the senses we have."

Another mother expressed her awakened sensitivity to others as a result of her having a child with a problem. "I have learned to be tolerant of people's short tempers. Who knows, maybe their son had a half-hour tantrum earlier — that could make anyone nervous."

One phone call taught me a valuable lesson in how to deal with other parents of children with problems. Mr. Smith called, very annoyed and upset because a member of PTACH's tuition committee had telephoned him at work and berated him for being late in his tuition payments. Mr. Smith was annoyed at being disturbed at his place of business, and even more, he was upset at the cold, business-like way in which he had been addressed. "You know, Mrs. Walburg, it is not easy having a child like Debra. We are very anxious about her development. You should tell your committee members that they should show some consideration for a parent's feelings. Such a man should certainly not be on a tuition committee. He does not appear to understand what we are going through."

I immediately empathized with Mr. Smith, and agreed that we parents deserve special kindness. I assured him that I would make certain such an incident did not occur again.

When I hung up, I investigated the story, and gently suggested to John, the member in question, that he try to be more sensitive when dealing with Mr. Smith and other parents.

"Well," John replied, somewhat indignant, "he can certainly afford the tuition. And he has some nerve not paying for two months. PTACH needs every dollar."

"I agree we need the money, but we can try and get it without hurting anyone — and I'm sure Mr. Smith just forgot to pay. He sounds extremely anxious about his daughter. He does not seem to have come to grips with her having a difficulty."

About two weeks later, I learned what Debra's difficulty was: she had a minor speech impediment. With less than a year's therapy, her problem was overcome. Yet Mr. Smith's distress had been real: for him, this imperfection in his child was overwhelming.

I often think of this story, and I've realized that in a sense Debra was less handicapped than her father. He had less strength; he needed a lot of understanding, support and sympathy. Debra just needed speech therapy.

Although I was president of PTACH for five years, I never spoke at any large function, except for the last one I attended. I recalled the story of Debra's father and spoke of a concept from the Bible, which enjoins us to be extra careful in our dealings with the orphan, the widow and the convert. The Torah uses these three examples which emphasize the need to be sensitive to the feelings of those most vulnerable. While it is true that we are always supposed to act with responsibility for our actions and words, we are cautioned to consciously proceed with extra sensitivity to those who need it. I pointed out that all parents are most vulnerable when it comes to their children, and advised that families with a handicapped child should be shown special consideration.

20

ON SHIMMY'S THIRD Purim since entering PTACH, he agreed to try on a costume and wear it long enough for me to take a picture of him. He went to synagogue to hear the *Megillah*, though he did not stay in the men's section the whole time. He came to me for some extra security. But Shimmy participated in Purim.

We were excited over little signs of Shimmy's growing awareness. One of his favorite subjects was *parashas ha-sha-vua*. This is the study of the weekly portion of the Torah read on the Sabbath in synagogue. Through this, Shimmy had learned of the Biblical disease *tzora'as*, a skin disease which afflicted those who told tales about others. Some time later, when a rash appeared on his arms, Shimmy clapped his hand over his mouth and exclaimed, "Uh-oh, I spoke *lashon ha-ra!*" This phrase literally means bad language: profane language, lies, slander, exaggerations are some of the categories of *lashon ha-ra* which we are cautioned against. Shimmy was seven or eight years old when this incident occurred, and we realized that he had shown comprehension of the concept of consequences for actions.

Shimmy has always been extremely afraid of dogs; he still is, most of the time. Once Yehoshua tried to reason with him: "Look, Shimmy — if a dog is barking across the street, it cannot hurt you. It's far away. Why are you afraid?"

"I don't like when dogs bark," replied Shimmy. "They don't speak English."

Yehoshua looked at Shimmy with surprise. "That's an interesting idea. People often fear things they cannot understand."

These two little anecdotes, in addition to making us laugh, served as a source of hope for us. Shimmy did think and relate to incidents. We found reassurance and proof that he was not so limited in intelligence.

21

ALTHOUGH WE LIVED in Carlton for six years, and PTACH was begun in our second year there, we never forgot our intention to return to Israel. It was always in our hearts and minds. But at this point we acknowledged the fact that what was preventing the fulfillment of our dream was not only our debt. We were worried about Shimmy.

After his first two years in PTACH, he showed definite improvement. He spoke without the gibberish that formerly filled in his sentences. He was slowly beginning to read English. He knew many Hebrew prayers by heart. Simple addition, until the number five, was mastered. In his third year in PTACH, he was able to join the regular second grade for *Chumash* — Bible study. With reinforcement in the PTACH class, he was actually learning to chant phrases from the Torah. Shimmy felt good about having a Rebbe — a male teacher, like other boys his age.

He had greater difficulty learning to read Hebrew than English. Reading Hebrew is most often taught with a phonetic approach: The letter *aleph* with a *patach* vowel under it makes an *ah* sound; the letter *beis* with a *patach* under it makes *bah*.

Since one of Shimmy's major learning disabilities was auditory processing, this method simply did not work for him. But when he was taught to see the letter and sound as one picture, it became easier, for Shimmy had a fairly good visual memory.

Thus, in light of his encouraging progress, we were reluctant to consider making a change. There was another factor as well affecting our possible move: PTACH had become my child too. I could not leave until I knew it was securely established. I knew that there is a general business principle which states that no one is indispensible. Yet, I also knew that there are times when a change in a fledgling organization can shake it up and weaken its structure.

PTACH had started out in September 1979 as one self-contained class of two little boys, and a resource room in Hebrew Academy with five boys. In January an urgent request was made by the principal of the girls' school for resource help — this from the man who, the previous June, had declared, "We have no children who need special education"! Our resource teacher divided her days between Hebrew Academy and the girls' school, a 15-minute drive away.

We had a wonderful volunteer principal, or educational supervisor — a retired assistant principal, Mrs. Brunner. She was always there, ready to substitute if our teachers were out sick.

By the time our second year came to a close, five boys had gone through the self-contained class. Two were Hebrew Academy students who were referred for intensive therapy in reading and math, and ultimately they were both mainstreamed back to their regular classes. The other two boys were newcomers to Carlton: a cheerful six-year-old with various learning disabilities, and a five-year-old who had a high IQ but was hyperactive and had various behavior problems. Shimmy was the fifth. It is interesting to note that despite the large Jewish population in Carlton, two-thirds of the self-contained full-day PTACH class was made up of children who had moved to Carlton specifically for our class.

Two grants to PTACH helped finance its second year. One of them was awarded for the next several years as well, which helped a great deal, both with the budget and with morale. I had helped write one of the proposals and found it a tremendous undertaking: it was like writing a major term paper! It turned out to be over twelve typewritten pages. I had to go to the library to do research on what constituted a proposal for a grant. In addition, the helpful people at the Associated Jewish Charities organization provided advice and guidelines. That first proposal had required such time and effort that it was a great relief when I finally mailed it out, and it was quite daunting when I got it back with questions for additional information!

By the end of PTACH's third year the program had grown greatly. The resource program in Hebrew Academy had trebled, and a second self-contained class — for two girls — had been formed. The girls' school resource program now included seven girls. We received a request from the *cheder* for the introduction of a speech therapy program for the coming year.

For its fourth year, PTACH was facing a budget of $75,000. At the board meetings, discussions were long and heated. Some members felt we could not increase our programs further; how would we pay for what we were already committed to? But I, as well as others, found it very difficult to tell parents there was no money for a program their child needed. I always argued that it is cost-effective to help the child when he is as young as possible, and I would optimistically assure my fellow members of the board, "Don't worry, money will come in somehow! These kids just cannot wait around until we have more money."

Since it ended up that I was the one who presented the prospective budget, I would always try to make it as rosy as possible, and try to minimize the deficit. God was helping us mothers and fathers: at the end of each year we found ourselves amazed — our teaching staff had been paid, materials had been purchased. We had made it.

Of course we did not rely on miracles; besides grants, tuition was collected. Fundraising projects were always going on. Bake sales were held at least three times a year, close to various Jewish holidays. We had an annual dinner; and we held a Judaica exposition, an exhibit and sale of Jewish art and gifts in which the artists paid to exhibit and gave us a percentage of subsequent sales.

For a few days before Passover, we would sell pizza, a wonderful convenience for mothers busy with the hectic preparations for the upcoming holiday. At Chanukah time we had a "package party," an auction for surprise gifts which were gaily wrapped. Twice a year we held bazaars or, as we advertised, "nearly-new sales." Special PTACH greeting cards were printed, which read: "A contribution has been made to PTACH in honor of ...", encouraging donations on special occasions. Greeting cards for Rosh Hashanah were also sold.

Each year we undertook new projects, and sometimes we dropped unsuccessful ventures. I would try to get a chairman or co-chairmen to volunteer for each project, assuring these volunteers that they could count on me for any assistance needed.

It worked out that we held a fundraising event about once every four to six weeks. In addition to this, the newsletter came out three or four times a year. Board meetings and educational committee meetings took place about once every six weeks.

All of these activities required the participation of someone who truly cared. I cared. I cared for Shimmy's sake and for the sake of Avram, Sari, Reuben, Lenny and all the children in the program, and their parents. Slowly, but very surely, other people in the Carlton community began to care too.

In March of 1983 Yehoshua got a call from a Principal of a girls' seminary in Jerusalem. The Rabbi wanted to interview him for the position of Director of a special second-year

seminary program for Orthodox young women in Israel. Yehoshua was quite flattered with the offer. Rabbi Hoffman had
done his homework well, and knew that we had plans to
return to Israel. He had heard of Yehoshua's expertise as an
educator and an administrator.

Yehoshua did not give him an answer right away. Although
we were in one way drawn to returning to Israel, we nevertheless had strong doubts about whether this was the right time
to go. Yehoshua was working on building up Hebrew Academy's dwindling dormitory population; he had also assumed
new responsibilities in Hebrew Academy's high school. PTACH
did not seem to be on a strong footing yet. Our most serious
consideration was that Shimmy did not seem ready. And so
we ultimately decided that we could not return to Israel — yet.

We needed to know, though, if Shimmy would ever be ready
to adjust to a new country and a new language. Yehoshua
sought advice from Rabbi Yaakov Kaminetsky (z"l), who was
the oldest great Talmud scholar in the United States at the
time. He was esteemed by all Jewry, throughout the world.
Besides being a very righteous and learned man, he was a
wise and understanding person with valuable insights into all
kinds of matters pertaining to everyday existence. Rabbi
Kaminetsky advised Yehoshua to delay our return to Israel
until Shimmy reached the eight-year-old level in his development. At that point he would have a firm grasp of the English
language. If we were to "change countries" earlier than that,
he felt, it would very likely confuse Shimmy and make it
difficult for him to communicate in both his mother tongue,
English, and his new language, Hebrew. Some time later we
discussed this advice with Shimmy's teachers, and they were
impressed with Rabbi Kaminetsky's recommendation. The
age of eight years, they told us, is considered a milestone in
the maturity of language and speech.

Close to Shimmy's eighth birthday I gave birth to our sixth
child, Tziona. We were all very excited about having another
girl in the family, and we named her Tziona as a reflection of

our strong desire to return to Israel — to *Tzion*. Fanny, her middle name, was given in memory of my great-grandmother. Somehow, Tziona's birth created less disruption to her siblings than had the birth of Yaakov. They would take turns holding their little sister, and when Shimmy's turn came, he was extremely gentle with her. Although Yona still maintained his resentment toward Yaakov, his younger brother, he seemed not to feel threatened at all by little Tziona. Yaakov himself was very interested — he had a little friend with whom he spent part of each day.

The summer Shimmy turned eight we enrolled him in Hebrew Academy's day camp, so that he would continue his association with the little boys he would be mainstreamed with during the year. I met with Shimmy's counselor before the program began and offered suggestions in dealing with Shimmy.

Positive reinforcement, I told her, is tremendously worthwhile. If Shimmy is praised for *davening* nicely he'll feel good and be more inclined to participate in other activities, too. Amy, Shimmy's PTACH teacher, also agreed to serve as consultant in case there were any problems. Shimmy needed to be told firmly what he had to do, and he had to know that the counselor expected him to behave like all the other boys. Although the camp director and Shimmy's counselor were apprehensive, they agreed to accept him.

On the first day I took Shimmy and introduced him to his counselor, and from the second day on Yosef and Shimmy ran over to Hebrew Academy every morning by themselves. Shimmy did not always want to play all the games; sometimes he cried when he felt he could not play as well as the other children. However, he slowly became a part of the group. He discovered that he was a powerful kicker and soon loved kickball.

At the end of the camp season Hebrew Academy had a color war. The camp was divided into two competing teams — each represented by a theme and a color. Shimmy proved to be a true asset to his team. He was quick to learn the cheers and marching songs. His team spirit was wonderful. Even if he garbled some words, his enthusiasm came across loud and clear and his singing rallied his fellow team members and they joined in. Shimmy was acknowledged the leader of "team spirit."

They just had to be sure to remind him not to sing along with the other team too!

22

IN THE SPRING of 1983, when Shimmy was almost nine, Yehoshua and I decided it was time for us to move out of the dormitory. We had been living there for five years, and the time had come to live in a normal house on a block with other Jewish families with children. We were fortunate to find a nice semi-detached house for rent on a small street in the heart of the Jewish community.

We were somewhat nervous about the adjustment for Shimmy and Yona. For one thing, any change could arouse anxiety in Shimmy. Also, the house shared a front lawn with the neighbors: Would the children realize that there were boundaries, areas where they could and could not go? On the Hebrew Academy campus they had unlimited space.

One psychologist I consulted suggested that I take the children to the house, walk around the yard, and while we walk, explain that we can only walk within a specific area. "Make it a game," she told me. "Tell them — Shimmy and the younger ones — that there is an invisible fence. They cannot see it, yet they cannot cross it. Teach them that the flowers in the next garden cannot be touched."

It sounded so simple — and, for once, it was! Yehoshua and I worried but the children readily accepted the new rules.

We also worried about how Shimmy would fare in a new *shul.* The community near Hebrew Academy was small and everyone was friendly with everyone else. Would Shimmy become overwhelmed by a larger place and a larger crowd?

Again our worries were unfounded. The people in the new congregation were warm and friendly, and many of the men were impressed with Shimmy's regular attendance, his decorum and fervent prayers. By the time Shimmy was nine he knew many of the prayers by heart. Though he still had trouble actually reading the Hebrew, he could find the place and chant the prayers.

Yehoshua has always taught our children that prayers should be expressed rather than just mouthed. Shimmy was a bit louder than necessary but his sincerity was apparent! Because he is such a good mimic, his intonations were quite appropriate — even if a bit exaggerated.

On the third Shabbos in our new neighborhood, I enjoyed some very special *naches* from my child: Shimmy was asked to lead the singing of *Adon Olam* at the end of the service. He proudly marched to the lectern and in a loud and melodious voice sang out the concluding prayer. Afterwards the men shook his hands and wished him "*Yishar ko'ach,*" as if he were one of them. It became a weekly ritual for Shimmy to sing this particular prayer; he knew all the words by heart and could handle it. There are other songs at the end of the service that were allotted to different little boys. These had more complicated sentences and Shimmy could not manage them.

The weekly singing gave Shimmy a special boost to his ego. He felt very important, and within a very short time he knew all the men and boys in *shul.* He felt like any equal member.

We lived in that house only one year. It was a very positive experience for all of us. Besides everything else, we lived near one of my sisters, and the cousins were able to visit each other often. When we moved there we did not realize it would be only for one year, but, as we say, *gam zo l'tovah* — this too was for the best.

There was only one aspect of our lives there that created an unpleasant experience: car pools! Because the public transportation in Carlton at the time was poor, people greatly depended upon car pools for transporting their children to and from school. Most of the children live in the city, and the Jewish school and yeshivas are all in the county, outside the city.

Our schedule was like this: Yehoshua left very early in the morning for Hebrew Academy. He had to be at the morning prayers there by 7:30 A.M. Yosef, already in junior high school, would go with Yehoshua. For Chaya, the car pool worked out very well. One of the mothers on the block taught at the girls' school and drove there every day. I rotated the afternoon car pool with three other mothers. Shimmy and Yona did not have to be in school until 8:40. They had a hard time getting up early. We bought a used station wagon so that I could participate in the car pools and also take the boys for therapy when necessary.

In the car pool, I had to drive nine children to school, two mornings and one afternoon each week. I would get up early and rush. Sandwiches were made the night before, so "all" I had to do was see that the children got dressed, ate breakfast, and left.

It never went smoothly. Yona proved to be the major problem. Already six years old, he nevertheless still had frequent "accidents." I would be out the door on the way to the car already, carrying Tziona to her car seat, when suddenly I would have to return home and change Yona's pants. Our mornings began to resemble the days when Shimmy was three, in Canada: I would now sit with Yona in the bathroom until the last minute, encouraging him to use the toilet. When it was my turn to drive, I would have to rush him out whether he had "made" yet or not. There were days when we would get into the car and suddenly, from the smell, I knew I would have to clean him up before taking him into class.

The mornings were full of tension. It was also hard for me to pick up the boys from the other three families and get them all to school on time. Even if I started earlier, Yona or sometimes Shimmy would create a problem the moment I was ready to leave. The other parents began to complain to me that it was not fair — I was making all their children late, the teachers were admonishing the children, and the children were upset. Less serious, but also unpleasant, was the teasing of some of the children when the car smelled bad.

I acknowledged that the mothers were right. I tried harder and got up earlier. Finally, towards the end of October, one of the mothers called me up. It was 8:30 A.M., she pointed out, and I still had not picked up her son. "You're out of the car pool!" she told me, politely but firmly.

Objectively, I could not blame her. Objectively, I knew I should not be angry at the other mothers. They were entirely justified, I told myself. Their children had to be in school on time. But, while I was able to control my anger, I was not able to control my feelings. I was very hurt. I felt rejected. I felt like a failure. I herded my children into our car and struggled to keep myself from crying. When I told the children what had happened, I realized that Shimmy and Yona and even little Yaakov felt hurt: they were no longer in a car pool like all the other children. I did not want them to feel unwanted, so I hid my feelings and announced, "You *are* in a car pool: the Walburg car pool! We take only Walburgs because we have so many. Now," I continued, "we don't have to rush as much in the morning. Isn't that great?"

They picked up my cue and began to feel better. And as their spirits lifted, mine did too. In fact I myself soon realized that the mornings were much less tense once we were out of the car pool. In fact, We even managed to get to school on time more frequently.

23

PURIM THAT YEAR was a lively and joyful experience for everyone. Shimmy went to *shul* on Purim eve with Yosef and
Yehoshua. As he heard the scroll of Esther being read, he kept
the place with his finger pointing in his *Megillah.* The following
day he donned a homemade paper crown and a cape made of
an old black skirt: Shimmy was King Achashverosh. He asked
me to draw a mustache on his face, and, taking little Yaakov
by the hand, they went off together to deliver *shalach manos*
to our neighbor two doors away. Shimmy decided it would be
nice to also bring a plate to our neighbors on the other side.
The Blums were an older couple and not Orthodox; other than
a polite hello, I'd had little to do with them. However, I was
proud of Shimmy's taking a friendly initiative and I happily
made up another plate of cake and fruit.

Shimmy was truly a good-will emmissary. Mr. and Mrs.
Blum were very appreciative. They became much more pleasant neighbors. Later in the day, Shimmy agreed to come in
the car along with several of the children as we went to deliver
shalach manos to friends who lived further away.

In the afternoon, we set up about 25 places for our Purim feast, adding to our dining-room table another long table extending the eating area into the living room. Quite a few boys from the Hebrew Academy joined us for the singing, the meal, and of course the obligatory wine-drinking. Shimmy sang along too. He had truly "learned" Purim.

24

WE CELEBRATED the Passover Festival in my sister Sheva's home. At the conclusion of the Seder, according to tradition, we loudly entreated the Almighty with: "Next year in Jerusalem." We spent the second half of the week of Passover in New York at my parent's home. As we visited many relatives and friends, we did not realize how true the age-old words "Next Year in Jerusalem" would be for our family.

After Pesach we came back to Carlton. I had not yet finished unpacking and washing all the clothes from the holiday, but I collapsed into bed and was already asleep when at 12:30 A.M. the phone rang.

Yehoshua quickly picked up the receiver as I wondered with some annoyance who could be calling so late.

"Hello! Hello!" he said. "Hello!"

A prank? I wondered.

"Hello! Yes, this is Rabbi Walburg speaking. Ah, Rabbi Solomon, *shalom aleichem* to you. Are you calling from Jerusalem?"

I was wide awake. Instinctively I felt that this phone call

was going to affect our lives.

"Well, yes," I heard Yehoshua reply, "of course I meant it when I said I hoped to return to Israel one year, soon."

As the conversation continued, I began to experience great anxiety. Yehoshua was being offered a job in a yeshiva in Israel. I knew this was a yeshiva which served a unique function and the job would be interesting and challenging. Before Yehoshua even hung up the phone, I somehow knew that next year we would, indeed, be in Jerusalem.

Yehoshua immediately realized I was nervous about the idea of moving to Israel at this time, and he tried to reassure me. "Nothing is definite yet, Rivka," he said. "First, I'll arrange a pilot trip to see the yeshiva first hand and decide if I want to work there. Rabbi Solomon also has to decide if he wants me. Then when I come back we'll discuss all the pros and cons. Don't worry."

Rabbi Solomon's phone call had come at the end of April. We all left for Israel in August, on the day after Tisha b'Av, the fast day which commemorates the destruction of the First and Second Temples in Jerusalem.

For Yehoshua there was the special enticement of a very desirable job. He would continue working in Jewish education as a Rebbe and a supervisor of post-high school young men. Moreover, he was not altogether sorry to leave his job at Hebrew Academy, where intra-school politics often created an uncomfortable atmosphere for him. His parents lived in Israel also, and it would be wonderful to be close to them again.

I hated the idea of moving anywhere, however. The thought of packing up again with our family of eight was loathsome to me, for we had just moved the year before. I felt very sad moving away from my sisters and all my family and friends. I was nervous about having to meet a whole new community and establish new relationships. And I would be leaving behind a "child": PTACH was already five years old and becoming well-accepted in the Carlton community.

I had to acknowledge that at this time PTACH could certainly survive without me. A professional fundraiser was being hired. A full-time principal would be running the educational programs. And many new capable volunteers were becoming involved with PTACH, both in fundraising and on the professional level. It was true: PTACH would do fine without me. But I would have a large gap in my life without PTACH.

Yehoshua and I spoke to each of the children about the "Big Move."

Yosef was a little frightened of the change but also welcomed the idea of no longer being "the principal's son." We had not realized to what extent this status had made him feel alienated from many of his classmates, since entering junior high school. Chaya was simply thrilled. She viewed the whole thing as one big adventure, and since she, like Yosef, had been born in Israel, she felt that she was going home.

Shimmy and Yona reacted very similarly. They each "agreed" to go, but stipulated it would only be for a visit. "I'll go, but then I want to come back to Carlton," Shimmy told us.

Yaakov and Tziona were really too young to have strong opinions on the subject. They only wanted to know if their cousins would also come.

Yehoshua explained to each of the children that living in *Eretz Yisrael* was a special privilege for us Jews, for God gave the Land to us. "*Imma* and I used to live there, and all these years we've been hoping we'd be able to return. We will live in Kiryat Ganim, a small town not far from Jerusalem with only religious families and lots of children. The people there are very friendly," he said. "We'll be able to see *Saba* and *Savta*, too. They live in Jerusalem, not far away."

Our last three months in Carlton passed in a blur. Yehoshua was busy tying up loose ends in the high school, and I worked on a detailed outline of all the projected PTACH activities for the coming year. Ruthy, Naomi and Mindy, the future co-presidents, and I set up committees to run each affair. I helped prepare the budget and recruited two volunteers to write up new proposals for grants. I met with the dinner and journal committees and was gratified that the plans were already in the process of being implemented.

Before we had come to a definite decision we decided it was imperative to find out if Shimmy was ready academically. We had a meeting with the PTACH principal. I asked her at what academic level Shimmy was performing. Based on an objective reading test and on the overall review of Shimmy's teacher, he was placed at a third-grade level. This evaluation was very important and gratifying. Rabbi Kaminetsky had recommended that we go only when Shimmy reached this academic age.

When one of the board members mentioned to me the idea of a goodbye party, I told them I would agree under a specific condition: It should be used as a fundraiser. The board planned the evening and invited Yehoshua and me as guests — but they did work out an angle to raise funds. I think they charged for participation.

An album was presented to us with many personal handwritten messages in it. There were various photographs including those from the last board meeting and from activities in the PTACH classroom. It is a beautiful memento which I cherish.

Partings are always hard, and this one was especially so. Many tears were shed when we left Carlton. We stayed in New York with my parents for several days until we left America. I find it hard to remember anyone else's feelings during those few days, for I was in a numbed state. Logically, I wanted to go to Israel. I knew this was where we belonged, but emotionally, I was very sad. There were so many people we were leaving in Carlton and in New York.

Yehoshua's excitement infected the children as well; moreover, they had new toys and books, and they were about to go on an airplane. I tried not to afflict anyone with my feelings and I just dealt with the packing, the last-minute shopping, and visits to friends and relatives. Being busy gave me little time to brood.

Our flight was very crowded, and there were many children aboard. Mine enjoyed the little trays attached to the seats — and Yona just couldn't keep from constantly pulling his down and putting it up, even during take-off. In fact, Yona was hyper much of the trip. I tried holding him on my lap to calm him down, but I was so tired I kept dozing off. I knew he was bouncing and squirming on me, but I was too tired to respond.

During our stopover in London, we had to follow El Al's very strict security rules. This meant we could leave the plane but we were restricted to a very small waiting room in Heathrow Airport. They allowed us to use the rest rooms but insisted on checking each passport and ticket upon our return to the waiting room.

Yona had no patience to wait in line with us while everyone's documents were being checked. He broke away and quickly ran to the barrier and crept under. Within seconds he was surrounded by three security guards with walkie-talkies and guns. Yona found this funny and began to laugh. So did I. I was tired, and punchy, and embarrassed, all at the same time. But I could not even stop laughing in order to answer immediately when one of the security guards starting yelling, "Whose child is this? Come and take him!" Yehoshua was still in the restroom. Luckily Yosef was sober enough to grab Yona's arm and pull him back to the line.

We arrived in Israel late in the afternoon. It took over three hours to process us as returning residents. Our luggage was checked, and papers were scrutinized. Yehoshua dealt with the bureaucracy while I dealt with the six children who just wanted to "go home" already. The AACI (Association of Americans and Canadians in Israel) provided drinks and snacks for us, as new *olim*, immigrants. The area where we waited was spacious, yet the children squabbled constantly. We were tired and all impatient to be on our way.

Finally, we piled our twenty-one boxes and suitcases, and seven pieces of hand luggage, onto seven or eight handcarts to wheel out of the airport terminal. The Jewish Agency had kindly provided a van to transport our luggage and most of the family to Kiryat Ganim. My father-in-law had come to the airport to greet us: He had waited for close to three hours! My mother-in-law was in our new house in Kiryat Ganim, making up beds and preparing supper for us.

As we walked out of the terminal we saw hundreds of Jewish people lining the area behind the barricades, smiling and waving — they were all waiting to welcome family and friends who were coming to Israel.

Shimmy was thrilled with the welcoming crowd, and assumed that they were all waving to him. So as he walked by, pushing the cart, he would stop, wave and bow his head in acknowledgment of the tribute he felt was being paid to him. He would raise his arms and wave, somewhat like a politician responding to his supporters.

This struck me as hilarious and I was laughing so hard that I could barely push my cart. Thus the luggage-traffic was seriously backed up by a waving and bowing little boy and his hysterical mother. Yosef, once again, maturely came to the rescue. He had finished bringing his cart to the van and hurried back to move us along. Yona kept running up and down the walkway, and did not seem to hear us calling to him. When a security guard yelled out, "Whose son is this?" another one answered, "Oh, that's just Yona." We seemed to have made an impression on the airport personnel.

Kiryat Ganim at last. It was nighttime when we arrived. We walked down the stone ramp leading to the semi-attached cottage that would be our new home. The house was made of pink and beige Jerusalem stone, and there was a large porch in front. It was very pretty and, I thought to myself, so different from any house in America.

Several of the wives of the Rebbes from the yeshiva had cooked food for us. The *Rosh Yeshivah*'s wife, Rebbetzin

Solomon, had personally supervised the moving in of beds for us all, and she had helped my mother-in-law make up the eight beds! All basic necessary furniture had been temporarily provided for us. We were all hungry and tired, but we had a lot to be grateful for that night.

25

SETTLING IN ISRAEL with six young children between the ages of two and twelve was a very different experience from coming alone as newlyweds. Unpacking and organizing a household for eight took time, but more significant was dealing with so many different people's feelings and emotions. Each child in his own way had to adjust to a new community, a new set of friends, a new language, a different school system and educational approach, transportation and lack of television. (Many religious communities and schools frown upon television viewing because of its negative and secular influence. We readily complied, and were even grateful for a definite way of breaking our children of the television habit.)

Yosef was twelve-and-a-half and had already begun learning to chant the portion of the Torah that he would read on his Bar Mitzvah. Although he knew Hebrew and in America he had been a straight-A student, now he suddenly found himself in a class of thirty-five Israeli children learning subject matter exclusively in Hebrew, and it was not easy. Yet, comparatively, Yosef had an easy time. Although he could not communicate fluently for at least six months, within a short time he was able to understand all the material. Yosef is the kind of person who does not readily express his feelings. There were times when he would hide in the bathroom and quietly cry from frustration. Only when I questioned him persistently would he let us know how much the language problem bothered him. But Yosef was fortunate to make several good friends who lived in Kiryat Ganim and were in his class. He was glad to be a student in a school where his father was not the principal.

Little Tziona was only two years old, and a couple of our next-door neighbors had little girls her age. They spoke a mixed English-Hebrew together, and Tziona easily became a little Israeli.

Yaakov was four, and also made friends with the neighbors quickly. However, for the first few months he was anxious about being accepted and he would run to give gifts to all of his new friends: toys and household items that we often had to retrieve, like a screwdriver, cups, wooden blocks, nails and more.

Chaya seemed at first to be adjusting well and easily. During our first month in Israel, before school started, she became friendly with one of the neighbors' daughters. But once school started, and shy, quiet Chaya entered a class of forty-six Israeli students, she was lost. She found the language very difficult, and it was hard for her to make friends with her Israeli schoolmates who seemed so different from her friends in America. Everyone warned me that adolescence is a difficult time for children and their parents, and eleven-and-a-half-year-old Chaya became progressively more unhappy as the months passed. Ultimately, we transferred her to a different Bais Yaakov school in the Jewish Quarter of the old city of Jerusalem. There the classes were smaller, with only twenty girls in her class, and at least a third of them spoke English. Although she definitely felt more comfortable in this school, nevertheless I found that there were constantly upswings and downswings in her moods.

An American teenager in Israel has to adjust not only to her own physical changes and mood swings, but also to the different social norms and customs of her Israeli counterparts.

For the first time in her life, Chaya had to wear a school uniform: a dark blue skirt and light blue blouse, the standard apparel of most of the Bais Yaakov students in Jerusalem. I was surprised to find that she absolutely hated the idea of a uniform, and suddenly became very interested in clothes. I was not prepared for this since, for the first ten years of her life, Chaya's wardrobe had consisted primarily of beautiful hand-me-downs — but hand-me-downs nonetheless — from a cousin's daughter. Chaya was never fussy and had worn whatever we received. Now everything had changed. Her discontent with life in Israel, like her general moods, would flare up and die down.

Yona had always been hard to figure out, and in our new environment this was certainly the case. He was disoriented but he would not tell us how he felt. He had frequent accidents in his pants. He began to wake up very early in the morning — before 5:00 A.M. — and sing! I often admonished him but Yona seemed to have no control over his singing. Although I became immune and was able to sleep right through it, unfortunately Mrs. Silver, our neighbor in the cottage below, never got used to the disturbance. I cannot blame her for that, and Yona's noise helped create an uncomfortable relationship with that particular neighbor.

Shimmy was the most open about his feelings. During the first week he cried and yelled, "I want to go home!", and would make phone calls on a toy telephone, to Grandma and *Zaidie* and to an older boy from Carlton whom he'd considered his friend. He would tell them on his phone that he did not like it here, and he wanted them to come to visit him. He wanted to go back. I felt so sorry for him.

Since school and yeshiva had not yet begun, I made a point

of taking the children to places outside of Kiryat Ganim so they could see a little of their new country. I took them to the zoo, to various sites in Jerusalem, to visit relatives, and, of course, to the *Kotel* — the Western Wall.

The children were all properly impressed at being by the very place where the *Beis Ha-Mikdash*, the Holy Temple, had stood.

I made a mistake, though, on our way home. I wanted to walk through the Arab market until Jaffa Gate, for I had found it to be fascinating when I had been in Israel as a student years before. I'd loved the many different little shops displaying colorful scarves, carved wooden camels and donkeys, woolen sheepskin coats and rugs, patterned leather bags and hassocks, bright brass vases, and all kinds of items you would certainly not find in America.

Chaya and Yosef were interested, but the three younger children were tired of walking. The worst thing was Shimmy's response: he became very frightened and anxious, and felt trapped by the narrow streets and dark alleyways.

"Oh no," he kept saying mournfully, "we'll never get out of here! I want to get out of here!"

We saw that our Shimmy, who had suffered such speech problems, was not only verbal about his feelings of fear and homesickness; his verbality served as a wonderful means of coping with the new environment. He would try to communicate with everyone. Of all the children, he was the first to actively use the Hebrew language, for he had the least inhibitions and did not mind at all making a mistake. And when he learned a sentence or a question he used it over and over again.

During the first few weeks, my in-laws came frequently from Jerusalem to visit.

"So, *Saba*," Shimmy would begin, "*mah shlomcha* — how are you? *Mah nishma* — what's new?"

And *Saba* would smile and reply in Hebrew, "*Ha-kol be'seder* — everything's fine."

Two minutes later Shimmy would repeat the question — and then two minutes after that. Each time *Saba* would patiently answer him. Shimmy was so enthusiastic about being able to greet people in Hebrew that he soon began greeting everyone he met in the street with a cheerful "*Mah shlomcha?*" He began picking up other sentences as well, and when he was stuck for a word he would simply make up one of his own! People would respond to him, to his eager friendliness, and if his statements were not always clear to them, it was simple enough to infer their meaning.

We were planning to send Shimmy and Yona to Limudei Hashem, the Israeli branch of the Orthodox special education school started by Rabbi Dr. Fried. Rabbi Fried had played a dominant role in its founding and operation during the first few years, and still continued his connection with the school and acted as educational consultant. Having made investigations in the United States and through my in-laws in Israel, I was confident that my boys would have a good school to attend. Although Yona was academically capable, he would have difficulties entering the mainstream, for he was hyperactive, knew no Hebrew, and still did not have total bathroom control. Shimmy, of course, needed special help to be able to learn.

Yehoshua had visited Limudei Hashem during his pilot trip to Israel, and registered the boys then. Shortly after our arrival I tried calling to confirm their acceptance to the school, but I was informed that since it was vacation time there would be no one to talk to until the day before school, when the staff returned.

It turned out that Shimmy and Yona did not start school until weeks after their siblings. This proved to be a terribly difficult time. Limudei Hashem was renovating their building and had to set up school temporarily in another location. The time needed to arrange the temporary classrooms had postponed the opening of school. When I was told that new students would be beginning yet several days later, I was absolutely furious. Every day that Shimmy and Yona were home, while the other children were in school, created tension.

I knew, though, that once they became involved in the routine of going to school every day, things would be much more comfortable. Waiting is never pleasant, and waiting for what I can only call the salvation of one's child is exceptionally difficult: proper placement for a child with special needs is in fact the child's salvation.

When finally the boys began going to school, transportation to and from Jerusalem became a new problem with which we had to contend. A special-education minibus transported children from Kiryat Ganim and the surrounding areas to various special schools in Jerusalem, but this school bus was already full for the present school year, so Yehoshua and I had to take Shimmy and Yona into Jerusalem every day ourselves. It was not easy.

We were able to arrange for transportation home for Yona at one o'clock in the afternoon. Shimmy finished school at four, and we solved the transportation problem by teaching him to travel home by himself. To go home he did not have to cross any busy streets. He got on a bus right in front of his school and got off at the Arab taxi stand where there was a taxi shuttle from Jerusalem to Abu Samil, a large Arab village next to Kiryat Ganim. Shimmy had become friendly with the taxi drivers when they drove into Kiryat Ganim to pick up passengers. I spoke to them and asked them to look out for him, which they happily did. In fact, several of them became Shimmy's good friends, and they called me *Imma shel Shimmy* — Shimmy's mother — and were particularly considerate to me because of their high regard for him. In addition to his growing Hebrew vocabulary, Shimmy now learned several Arabic greetings.

Within a few months we were settled in. Yehoshua and I

marveled that it had taken four long years for Shimmy to learn to speak his mother tongue, English, and only four months to become fairly fluent in a new language, Hebrew.

The Talmudic expression *Avira d'Eretz Yisrael machkim* — "The air of Israel causes one to be wise," seemed to apply to Shimmy. He was learning many things.

26

CHANUKAH TIME was approaching. One day I received two urgent messages from Limudei Hashem. One note urged me to attend an emergency meeting for parents, and the second note informed me that the school would be closing one day early for Chanukah. The teachers were striking.

I was concerned and sorry that Shimmy and Yona would be missing another valuable day of school, yet, selfishly, I was excited by announcement of the parents' meeting. I had wanted to become involved with the school. After my total involvement with PTACH I missed being active. At the beginning of the year, I had offered the assistant principal my services in any capacity she felt would be useful, but no one had called on me. Now, perhaps, I would find a way to become helpful.

At the meeting I learned that Limudei Hashem was a ship adrift without a captain. The current principal had just left the country for emergency medical treatment, and the assistant principal was on maternity leave. No one had assumed the responsibility of seeing that the teachers' salaries would be paid, and when the staff sought their wages they were consistently referred to different individuals who gave them no assurance that they *would* be paid. The staff as a group and as individuals had impressed me as being very dedicated and caring. Their going on strike was unprecedented and very surprising. But when I learned a little about the history of the school, I understood their reaction to the present crisis and I could not fault them.

When Limudei Hashem was founded, an American businessman undertook to finance it. When the diamond industry took a plunge, this benefactor was seriously affected. The dedicated staff continued to work for *nine months* without pay. Several of the teachers incurred serious debts while struggling to feed their families. Eventually — after several years — the teachers were compensated. Understandably, the staff was not prepared to undergo such hardships once again. They felt there was no one to turn to, no one who would accept the responsibility for seeing they got paid. They called for a vote of action. There was a lot of dissension, and the decision to strike was reached with much regret. They would strike and thus call attention to the serious financial plight of the school. The strike was a plea to the parents to get involved.

Rabbi Greenberg, a *Rosh Yeshivah* of an established Israeli yeshiva, was chairman of the board of directors. Mr. Shlossberg, a notable businessman, was treasurer. A respected Sephardic Rabbi, a Dutch businessman, and another father had formed a non-profit corporation for Limudei Hashem whose purpose had been to raise money for renovating the school building; now, they assumed a new role — that of the financial administration of the school. At the open meeting for parents, Rabbi Greenberg explained the gravity of the school's financial state, and made it clear that unless the teachers could be guaranteed a salary the school would have no choice but to close. The parents were being appealed to, to seek sources of funding.

"We need more parents involved," said Rabbi Greenberg.

"Who will join our board of directors?"

Yehoshua and I immediately raised our hands. We looked around to see who else had, and discovered that although there were more women than men among the twenty-five parents present, I was the only female to have raised her hand. One Jerusalem mother loudly exclaimed to her neighbor, "What can women do? How foolish!"

When the meeting came to an end, I turned to a group of women and said, "Women can do a lot to raise funds: we can organize bazaars and dinners."

"Yes," replied one, "women can raise money — but it should be done separately from men. A woman doesn't belong on a board with men."

"Why not?" I hotly replied. "In Carlton I was very involved on a board of men and women."

"Oh, America!" she said deprecatingly. "This is Jerusalem." I decided not to say anymore, but to attend the next meeting of the board — even if they thought I was coming just to accompany my husband.

I always smile now when I recall that first board meeting I attended, on the Saturday evening which followed the one-day strike.

The board members were a formidable group. Rabbi Greenberg, a Slonim chassid, was dressed in his traditional Shabbos clothes: a long black coat and a round brown fur hat — a *shtreimel.* Mr. Schlossberg, a Ger chassid, wore traditional black trousers gathered under the knee, a long black coat, and a black square fur hat — a *spudik!* Rabbi Dr. Fried, a Munkatch chassid, had flown in from America for emergency consultation. He too wore a long black coat, and his large round reddish brown fur *shtreimel* matched his beard. Also present were a Vizhnitz chassid in full garb, the Dutch businessman and Sephardic Rabbi I'd met before, Yehoshua — and I! I knew Hebrew but my speech was not so fluent. More than my insecurity in the language, I was very much cowed by being the only woman present at this impressive gathering. I barely spoke — but I listened well.

As I listened, I came to realize that while I might sit on the board, I could never fulfill a role in Limudei Hashem the way I had in PTACH. Being a woman limited me. The woman at the parents' meeting was right: this was Jerusalem. Moreover, I was not at the stage in my life where I could spare so much time for the school. Israel had different ways, different bureaucracy, different methods from America. I was not ready then to learn from scratch what needed to be done. My family needed my presence and support in adjusting to life in Israel. I needed more time at home, for all the cooking and baking that life in Israel entailed.

Every Friday night we had a get-together — an *Oneg Shabbat* — in our home for the boys from the yeshiva. Living in Israel had new demands on my time, and living in Kiryat Ganim, outside of Jerusalem, also made it more difficult. I did not have a car at my disposal and could not "run around" the way I had done in Carlton. School and nursery school finished for some of the children as early as 12:30, and I had to be home. I accepted the fact that at different stages in one's life one was capable of doing different things.

The Ladies' Auxiliary of Limudei Hashem became a viable organization. Once again I experienced the pleasure of being involved in a charitable organization, and of one of the fringe benefits: I met and made friends with many wonderful women. Among the women involved were parents of children with difficulties and people who were simply interested in helping. My life was enriched by the newly formed friendships with these women from England, Switzerland, Austria and other countries.

At our first ladies' meeting we decided that we would set two goals: to help the school financially, and to try to increase awareness in the general community of the needs of the many children with learning difficulties.

Our first fundraising event was held on the first day of Adar, the Hebrew month corresponding most closely to March, in which Purim is celebrated. There is a Hebrew saying which states, "When Adar comes in, we increase our joy." And so we did. A ladies' evening of tea and cake took place in a hotel in Jerusalem. Close to six hundred women attended and we brought in over $6,000 profit. It was a successful evening from all accounts. The guest speaker was a very interesting person: a Rabbi who was a ba'al teshuvah, a former secular Jew who had become religious later in life. Formerly he had been a famous Israeli comedian, a television and movie star. A highly intelligent man who had sought to understand more about his heritage and had subsequently become immersed in Torah study, this charismatic Rabbi held the audience's attention as he encouraged parents to accept their children as gifts from God. "None of us know what is in store for us, what the future holds," he told us, clearly referring to his own life which underwent such unexpected changes.

The Ladies' Auxiliary also held bazaars and sales, but these required much work and brought in small profits. After a year we arrived at the decision to leave aside all of the small projects, and we began holding yearly dinners — exclusive evenings for women. We found that this brought in a substantial sum of money for the school, and our dinners gained the reputation of being worthwhile and interesting events, featuring a top program about special education. Thus the annual dinner became an event eagerly anticipated all year by a large and growing crowd of women.

Although I remained on Limudei Hashem's board and occasionally had the opportunity to express an opinion, I felt truly useful as a member of the newly established Ladies' Auxiliary.

The adjustment of the Walburgs became complete. By our first Chanukah, I had already begun to be immersed in the

Ladies' Auxiliary of Limudei Hashem; Yehoshua was enjoying his role in the yeshiva as both Rebbe and advisor; Yosef celebrated his Bar Mitzvah; Chaya celebrated her Bas Mitzvah; Yaakov learned to read Hebrew in preschool; and he and Tziona developed Israeli accents in Hebrew as well as in English. Shimmy and Yona had accepted their new routines and schools.

Yosef's Bar Mitzvah was exciting — our first *simchah* to be commemorated in Israel. My parents, a brother, and three sisters all came in from the United States for the happy occasion. On the actual day of his birthday, we invited many friends and relatives to a festive dinner in his honor.

On Shabbos, Yosef read the whole *parashah*, the weekly portion of the Torah. We made a big *kiddush* after the morning service. Yosef had read the Torah beautifully, and we wanted to include the whole congregation in our joy at this occasion. Our extended family ate lunch together afterwards and Yosef delivered a Talmudical dissertation during the meal.

Shimmy, as always, enjoyed the partying. After Shabbos he posed for a picture in Yosef's new black hat, a symbol of his status as a Jewish "man," and began to make plans for his own Bar Mitzvah. He could not wait to wear a hat.

Our first Purim in Kiryat Ganim was very special: Shimmy brought a gorilla to our house — or, rather, a boy dressed up as one! One father in our community, a teacher in the *cheder* who was a friendly, affectionate person, played the guitar and was much loved by all the children of Kiryat Ganim. That Purim morning, I was busy sending out *shalach manos*, and Shimmy — dressed in a bathrobe, a crown, and a painted-on mustache — was out delivering plates of goodies to his friends. There he met Rebbe Dovid and joined his Purim entourage. The Rebbe was playing his guitar and singing. He was the pied piper of Kiryat Ganim: all the costumed children had joined him, including one tall anonymous gorilla.

I heard the joyous singing moments before I saw the group. I ran out to the front porch and there I saw Shimmy actually holding a furry hand! Shimmy, who used to be so fearful of strange new things, and, I never forgot, of Purim especially. The next thing I knew they had marched up our front steps onto the porch, gone into the house, and had danced around the dining-room table, singing and making merry.

I quickly tried to give out some *hamantashen* treats to the children, but they were already rushing off to dance at the next house. It was beautiful beyond words — all the children so full of Purim joy — and Shimmy was part of it.

27

SHIMMY'S FIRST YEAR in Limudei Hashem proved very successful. His exceptional teacher, Tova, and her excellent teaching
assistant, appreciated Shimmy's strong desire to learn. Realizing that motivation was not his problem, Tova tried various
methods to teach him to read Hebrew. She encouraged him
to use his strong visual memory in order to acquire a fund of
Hebrew words.

Actually Shimmy had been learning English with this
method and, although Hebrew is seldom taught non-phoneti-
cally, for Shimmy the sight method was best. Shimmy's
teachers used behavior modification in all aspects of his
education. They rewarded him with stickers and points that
accumulated and led to bigger prizes. Shimmy loved to receive
prizes but never kept them, always giving the little cars or toys
to one of his younger siblings. This is very characteristic of
him: he has always liked to give presents and seldom wants
things for himself.

Yona also flourished in his year at Limudei Hashem and by
June was speaking Hebrew like a native Israeli. He was still

hyperactive, and took the medication Ritalin, a drug which helped him concentrate and remain seated in class. With Yona it was immediately apparent that Ritalin was a suitable solution for him. When he took it, he behaved in class; after four hours, when the drug wore off, he would begin to fidget.

I spoke to the family doctor in Kiryat Ganim and decided that Yona would continue to take Ritalin twice a day, as he had in the United States. When Yona was four-and-a-half, a doctor in Carlton had recommended the medication, but I was extremely reluctant to "drug" my child. Nevertheless, I felt that I should at least look into the subject. I went to the library and took out several reference books about medication, and I also looked for articles about hyperactive children.

I learned that all the available data on the effects of Ritalin pertained to children six years of age and older. The side effects included loss of appetite, sleeplessness, and the slowing down of growth. All of the side effects are immediately reversible when the medication is stopped. One doctor explained that the child's slowed-down growth is not the direct result of the Ritalin itself, but rather of his eating less and sleeping less, which affect his natural growth process. To counteract this, I was advised to give the Ritalin only on school days. On weekends, holidays and summer vacations no medicine should be given.

When he reached the age of six, I decided to start giving him the Ritalin. If Ritalin was appropriate for him, it would be apparent almost immediately. The drug takes effect within fifteen minutes and a noticeable calmness in the child can be seen. Of course, the exact dosage has to be found. When too little was given to Yona he remained hyper. When even a little too much was given, he became a bit "spacey" — "out of it." The usual dose ranges from 5-10 mg. Yona took 5 mg. for a year and then went up to 7 1/2 mg.

Ritalin is a strictly regulated drug both in the United States and in Israel. It works as a stimulant for adults and is considered a narcotic. In Carlton, I could get a prescription good for only 30 days; in Israel, the prescription is good for only 10 days — and only one pharmacy in Jerusalem carried the drug. The family doctor at Kiryat Ganim trusted my handling of the medication and would prescribe the maximum amount allowed for a child, for 10 days. Thus I could give Yona only what he needed, but by getting more pills it saved me special trips to Jerusalem.

When Yona was eight-and-a-half, a neurologist suggested that we try stopping the medication during a school day to see if Yona still needed it. Children approaching adolescence, he explained, sometimes outgrow the need. At that time I was sure that Yona still needed the pill but reluctantly I agreed to experiment for a day or two.

After only half a day, one of his teachers called to ask if we had forgotten to give Yona his pill. I explained that the doctor wanted to see how Yona would behave without it. The teacher told me that Yona was not sitting still; he was laughing a lot; and in general, he was being very disruptive. She agreed to try another day but made it clear that she did not think taking Yona off the medication was a good idea.

I agreed with the teacher and decided not to waste another day. When Yona was on Ritalin it calmed him down physically — and I'd seen that if I was able to keep him entertained or busy with something he enjoyed, he would remain calm even after the effects of the pill had worn off.

One neurologist I spoke with felt it was wise to give a hyperactive child Ritalin 3 times a day, 7 days a week, until he reached adolescence. His theory was that if the child acts "normal," people will react well to him, and the child would develop a positive self-image. He would never encounter reactions of anger and disgust that hyperactive children often meet. He would simply feel good about himself, and when he grew older and was no longer dependent on Ritalin for controlling his hyperactivity he would be like any other child.

Athough the doctor's theory *sounded* good, I did not consider it realistic. In the case of Yona (and many children on

Ritalin), when he took a pill late in the day, after 3:00 P.M., he would not be able to fall asleep until very late at night. Children have to sleep in order to grow and develop, and Ritalin given late in the day definitely interfered even more with his normal sleep pattern.

The school year was over at the end of June, but Limudei Hashem had a three-week summer progam that included some learning, prayers, and other structured activities.

I initially worried about what Shimmy and Yona and, in fact, all the children would do during the rest of the summer. But my worry was needless — Kiryat Ganim is a wonderful place for children. There are wooded areas, where a child cannot really get lost but can feel that he is in the middle of the forest. He can build tree houses, play hide-and-seek, find turtles and lizards — as well as cats and dogs. Children can ride their bicycles in the streets of our village and not have to worry about traffic. The central playground has shade and sun and lots of sand.

During the summer vacation, Shimmy proved to be my least concern. He rose early every morning and went to morning prayer services in one of the yeshivos. Afterwards he would join the young men from the yeshiva for breakfast and then he would go and sit in the study hall with a tome open before him, and "learn." What he learned I do not know but he loved being in that environment.

We also took a short family vacation and went for two relaxing days to a small town near the sea whose boarding school is empty in the summer. The dormitory rooms are rented out to religous families. Meals and swimming facilities are provided. Yosef and the younger boys went swimming with the men, while Chaya, Tziona and I went swimming with the women, either to the separate beach in nearby Ashdod or to the swimming pool in the religious kibbutz Chofetz Chayim. Yehoshua was delighted to be able to sit in on lectures and join study groups. Shimmy spent hours in the community's *beis midrash* — the house of study. He was not interested in going swimming, and he was perfectly content being left to his own devices. Of course he immediately made friends with the men who were sitting and learning, or praying, in the *beis midrash.*

During his eleventh year Shimmy continued to attend Limudei Hashem for a full day. Yona also attended until four o'clock during that second year in Israel. Shimmy, the big brother, took Yona home every day, and although it was good for him to feel responsible, he sometimes became too bossy. Shimmy acted like a strict parent and would smack Yona if he didn't hurry along. They often fought, and I would look at them and think of a cartoon of a dog chasing a cat chasing a mouse.

Our seventh child and fifth son was born in our second year in Kiryat Ganim. Shlomo was born during the Festival of Sukkos. He was a little small, but thank God, a healthy, cute baby who immediately became the favorite plaything of all his siblings. Shimmy would gently rock him, Yona would walk him in the carriage, and all would fight for turns to hold him.

When Shimmy turned twelve in the summer Yehoshua and I sat down to discuss his upcoming Bar Mitzvah that would be the following year. Since Shimmy loves to sing and he has been blessed with a beautiful, resonant voice, I kept thinking how nice it would be if he were able to recite the entire portion of the Torah on the Shabbos of his Bar Mitzvah. But Yehoshua realistically suggested, "First let him prepare the *Haftarah*, and after he masters that, we'll see what we can actually expect."

The *Haftarah* is a section of Prophets recited each Shabbos. It can be read from a regular large printed book, with all the pointed vowels and cantillation markings. It is also much shorter than the Torah portion, and all in all much easier to learn. (When reading from a Torah scroll the letters do not include the vowels or the cantillation marks, and the reader has to learn them by heart.)

We knew Shimmy would have little trouble learning the melody, but we were rightly concerned about his reading accurately and about clear articulation. First of all, we needed to find someone to teach him. Yehoshua, though qualified as a *ba'al koreh* — one who reads the Torah, did not have the time to work with him consistently. In addition to all his other responsibilities at the yeshiva, he had recently begun to make trips to the United States several times a year, to recruit students and to raise funds.

The fact is, though, that even if Yehoshua had had the time, we realized that it would not be a positive experience for Shimmy to have his father teach him. Although Yosef had been able to learn from his father, with the help of a tape Yehoshua made for him, we knew that with Shimmy it would not go so easily. As I learned many years before, a parent is not always the best teacher for his child.

We decided to wait until the school year began and see if we could arrange for him to learn with a Rebbe in school. Yehoshua felt that if it looked like it would be a problem then Shimmy could forgo reading aloud altogether — all he actually had to do for his Bar Mitzvah was to be called up to the Torah and recite a blessing on the section of the Torah to be read. He didn't have to be the one to read it.

I strongly disagreed with Yehoshua. I felt that a simple *aliyah* — being called up — was not enough at all. Shimmy was capable of learning at least the *Haftarah*, and he should therefore do it. It would give him a trememdous feeling of self-worth, of being able to do what all his friends and his brother could do. I was determined Shimmy would succeed.

At the end of August the new students began to arrive at the yeshiva. Among them was a special young man named David. An excellent *ba'al koreh*, he had learned to chant from the Torah from an exacting teacher. He was gifted with a sweet and melodious voice and that, together with his meticulousness in chanting the Torah, made him seem like a good candidate for teaching Shimmy.

David was attracted to yeshiva study, but like many of the beginning students, found he did not have patience to sit and learn for too many hours at a time. He was musically gifted and preferred playing his guitar to learning.

Yehoshua approached David with the project of teaching Shimmy for his Bar Mitzvah. David was very enthusiastic; it sounded to him like a wonderful challenge.

The first session with Shimmy went well. They spent a few minutes getting acquainted, and briefly reviewing the blessings recited over the Torah. Shimmy was familiar with these *berachos* because they are repeated each week on Shabbos in *shul,* and he had also heard Yosef practicing them during his Bar Mitzvah year. However, though Shimmy knew the general tune, he was not clear on all the words. David was pleased with the results of the first session. I thanked David profusely and gave him a batch of brownies.

David came back full of enthusiasm to a second lesson that did not proceed well at all.

"That's all for today!" Shimmy declared after the first two minutes.

"But, Shimmy! We just started," said David in amazement.

Shimmy quickly grew angry. "I said that's all! That's all is that's all. No more!"

When I heard Shimmy beginning to shout, I rushed in. "Why are you yelling?" I asked. I did not want him to scare David away.

"*Imma!* That's all. I told him that's all. No more today!" he yelled.

"All right, Shimmy, calm down. If you don't want to practice today, you can practice more on another day," I said.

"No! No! I don't want to. I'm getting out of here." He was beyond reasoning with. "I don't like this!" He stormed out of the room.

I wanted to reassure David, who was bewildered. "Listen, David, don't be upset. It's certainly not you he's angry at. He's just reacting to what he feels as the pressure of the new situation. He needs to get used to the idea of studying new material and mastering it. It will be all right. I'll ask my husband to talk to him after he's calmed down," I told David. "Want a cookie before you go?"

"No, it's okay. Don't worry, I'll give it another try — if he'll let me."

When Yehoshua came home he told me that David had already come to him with a report of the day's lesson. Yehoshua spoke privately to Shimmy, encouraging him to continue studying since we all knew that he would be able to do a beautiful job. He also warned Shimmy that he was required to be respectful to David, since David was now his Rebbe.

The afternoon program in Limudei Hashem was to start after Sukkos. Yehoshua and I decided that we would send Shimmy only half a day that year — to just the morning program. I wanted Shimmy to learn happily, without pressure. Learning with David late in the day would have been more difficult. For David, it worked out well, too. Two o'clock in the afternoon was a convenient time for him to come to the house.

The Bar Mitzvah lessons progressed. Though Shimmy actually spent only a little over an hour a week studying, divided into three sessions, to him it seemed like more. He sometimes felt pressured.

I became aware of the degree of concern and anxiety he felt about his Bar Mitzvah when one day he came to me and said, "You know what, *Imma*, I feel like cancelling the whole thing. Let's forget about this Bar Mitzvah."

"Why?" I exclaimed in surprise.

"I just feel like cancelling it, that's all."

"But you'll have so much fun, Shimmy. And you'll get a lot of presents too. Grandma and *Zaidie* are coming from America, and Uncle Tzvi and Uncle Ari. We're all going to be so proud of you," I said. "And we know you'll chant beautifully."

"You know what, *Imma*, let's just tell them not to come!"

I wasn't sure how to answer him so I said, "Well, let's ask *Abba* what he thinks."

Yehoshua and I decided we would just see how Shimmy felt, with the passage of time. One Shabbos after morning prayers, Shimmy came home with a pocket full of candy.

"Where did you get all that candy, Shimmy?" I asked.

"Shmuli Cohen had a Bar Mitzvah today. When they called him up to the Torah, everybody started throwing candy," he answered, beginning to laugh. "It was so funny. They were trying to knock off his new hat. I picked up all these candies from the floor. You know, *Imma*, when I have *my* Bar Mitzvah, I'm going to take off my hat so they won't get it."

I was so happy to hear Shimmy planning his Bar Mitzvah again. Though he had his moments of nervousness, he began to anticipate the event more positively. As time went on and he knew the *Haftarah* better, he felt more confident in his own ability. I realized though that his reading the entire portion of the week was simply a fantasy of mine, and not possible. But I was happy with his progress in learning the *Haftarah*.

David persevered all year. We were so sorry when we learned that he would not be able to be at Shimmy's Bar Mitzvah. The yeshiva program ended in June and David had to return to the United States for a job: he needed to work during the summer to finance a second year of Torah study in Israel.

Somewhere during Shimmy's twelfth year we realized that Yona was undergoing a definite learning spurt. He was a little over nine years old at the time. It seemed that suddenly he knew how to read Hebrew fluently, with or without the vowels under the letters. We became aware that he could even read the small medieval Hebrew script of Rashi's Bible commentary which appeared at the bottom of the page of his *Chumash*.

My mother-in-law called me up after Yona had spent a Shabbos there. "Rivka, are you aware that Yona reads from the Torah beautifully?" she asked me. "I'll bet he's ready to go to a regular school already. He might have needed a special program when he first came, but I don't think he does anymore. You should look into it."

We had always thought that Yona would eventually go to a regular *cheder* — we just never knew when he would be ready. It is always easier to wait until the school or someone official and professional tells you, and no one had yet. However, my mother-in-law's prodding did cause me to look at Yona afresh.

Yona liked to know things. He liked answering the questions on the weekly *parashah*, and on laws relating to Shabbos and Festivals. He liked reading the Bible. We hired a Rebbe to teach him *Chumash*, for in Limudei Hashem, at that time, the boys were taught only a summary of the weekly portion and a few sentences from inside the text. With the private Rebbe, Yona was learning, in the *cheder* style, a whole *parashah* of text and commentaries. Within a month, he surprised the Rebbe with his comprehension and retention. He caught the rhythm of learning and was doing well.

More and more, Yona's going to a regular *cheder* seemed like a realistic idea. I asked the Rebbe to now introduce Yona to the learning of Mishnah — this is the next step in the progression of topics learned in boys' schools. Once again Yona proved to have an aptitude for learning; within a month the Rebbe was able to discern his comprehension and ability to learn Mishnah. He was not a genius but he showed good potential.

We were not sure how to proceed, not sure what class he should go into. We were sure he was not ready to enter a class with boys his age, for the children there had been learning *Chumash* and Mishnah for several years, and they were already learning Talmud — the next step.

We consulted once again with a child psychologist who recommended we go to Rabbi Shammai Gross, a Rebbe with excellent educational skills and talents. He had worked as a special educational Rebbe in Limudei Hashem, and was now working as an educational advisor in a regular *cheder* in addition to working on special education projects.

He taught and then tested Yona, and strongly recommended placing him in a regular school, in fourth or even fifth grade, only one year behind his age level. Our impressions, as parents, were justified. The report made me glow.

Our living in a small community served us well at this time. Most *cheder*s are not prepared to accept children who have been labeled as "special." But the Kiryat Ganim Talmud Torah was built to serve the children of the Kiryat Ganim community. Yona could not be offhandedly refused. The principal was concerned but sympathetic, and he accepted Yona.

In the summer of Shimmy's Bar Mitzvah two milestones were met. Shimmy reached Jewish manhood. Yona left behind a label.

Yehoshua made a trip to the United States in the spring before the Bar Mitzvah. I measured Shimmy as best as I could and asked Yehoshua to try and get him a Bar Mitzvah suit while he was there. This was not an easy matter: Shimmy was less than five feet tall, and very heavy. A man's size shirt fits his girth, for example, but the sleeves are way too long.

My parents found a suit — men's stout size. They picked out a tie too and sent it all back with Yehoshua. The jacket fit fairly well, although the sleeves needed shortening. The pants were ridiculously long and even a little tight. A competent tailor let them out and even added a little material to make them wider.

Shimmy loved best trying on his new hat. He looked so cute — like a little man. Second to *tefillin*, it is the most overt sign of the change in status of a Bar Mitzvah boy, in our circles.

Yosef had begun to put on *tefillin* one month before his Bar Mitzvah, according to our custom. But with Shimmy, Yehoshua was not certain how to proceed. (A set of *tefillin* consists of two small square leather boxes which contain Scriptural portions handwritten on parchment. They are worn on the left arm and the forehead, by Jewish males aged 13 and over, during morning weekday prayers. *Tefillin* are considered very holy and a certain decorum is required when wearing and handling them.) Shimmy still wet the bed occasionally and his dexterity was not the greatest: What if he dropped them? Yehoshua went to a *posek* — an ordained Rabbi who is qualified to answer questions that arise about Jewish law.

Yehoshua told the *posek* about Shimmy's problems. "In light of these," he asked, "how should I proceed to prepare Shimmy for putting on *tefillin?*"

The *posek* made a very practical suggestion. He lent Yehoshua a pair of *tefillin* that were not perfect and therefore considered not kosher. A blessing could not be made on them. Yehoshua taught Shimmy how to put on *tefillin* with the unkosher set, and had him practice every day.

It was difficult for Shimmy to get the configurations of the straps right. All the boys have to be shown more than once, and all the boys need to practice. For Shimmy it was even more difficult. He would get frustrated easily and make mistakes, but he kept trying. Sometimes when he woke up very early, he would go to *shul* before Yehoshua or Yosef were up and able to help him. He would then ask someone in *shul* for help.

We constantly stressed to Shimmy that his pants had to be clean if he wanted to wear *tefillin,* for *tefillin* are very holy. When reciting any prayer, or at the mention of God's name, we have to be clean. For *tefillin* the same rule applies. Shimmy understood that he had to be extra careful. The doctor in Kiryat Ganim prescribed a medication to be taken at night, which would help Shimmy maintain bladder control. In Carlton, Shimmy had taken this at one time and it had been effective. In fact, when he had stopped taking it, he had remained dry for a long time. Now, when the bedwetting again became a problem, I asked our local doctor if he felt Shimmy should resume taking it. I told him how staying dry at night had carried over to the day. He agreed, and prescribed the medication. The incentive of the new *tefillin* that his grand-parents had bought him also made Shimmy more aware and careful about this problem.

Shimmy's Hebrew birthday fell on a Sunday. We held a reception in his honor in the front yard of the yeshiva in Kiryat Ganim where Yehoshua was Rebbe. Shimmy had made up a list of his own, of people to invite. Besides all the boys from his class and his Rebbeim and teachers from Limudei Hashem, he had another whole group of friends: all the members of the Chassidic *shul* at Kiryat Ganim, where Shimmy liked to pray. Yehoshua did not even know them all!

Originally, we thought to invite primarily friends and rela-tives who live outside of Kiryat Ganim and who would not be able to come to the *kiddush* on Shabbos. We, however, were happy to change this plan and agree to Shimmy's wishes.

A *mechitzah*, a partition, was put up to separate the men's and women's tables. Lanterns were strung and two spotlights were borrowed to light up the area. The cook from the yeshiva prepared salads, knishes and meatballs.

I had spent several weeks baking dozens of cakes and batches of cookies. My freezer was full to capacity with homebaked goods.

We asked someone to play the keyboard, wanting music to set the tone of a joyous occasion. As it turned out, though, we did not have to have the music at all. All of the guests present felt the *simchah*, the happiness. There was continual singing and dancing on the men's side.

At Yosef's Bar Mitzvah there had been four speeches: Yehoshua, his father, my father and Yosef all spoke. At Shimmy's Bar Mitzvah there were no formal speeches. Shimmy, on his own initiative, took the microphone from the musician and spoke spontaneously: "I want to thank everyone for coming, my grandparents from America and *Saba* and *Savta* and *Bubby* and Aunt Sue and Uncle Chaim and Ari and Tzvi from America, and *Morah* Amy. It says in the Torah you have to respect your parents and now that I'm a Bar Mitzvah I have to be sure to have *Kibbud Abba Ve'Imma*, respect for my parents. Thank you all for coming, and have a good time!"

He was so cute, a little man in his hat and suit, greeting and thanking his guests. *Morah* Amy, his teacher from PTACH in Carlton, had come to Israel with her family for a six-week visit. They had come to celebrate with us Shimmy's Bar Mitzvah. Dan, Amy's husband, made a video of the Bar Mitzvah.

When we watched it afterwards I could see that Shimmy had been quite nervous. He kept licking his lips throughout the evening, between singing, speaking, and eating. I do not remember seeing him ever lick his lips other than that night.

Shimmy's Bar Mitzvah week was hectic, but fun. Sunday evening was the reception. On Monday morning he got his first *aliyah* — calling up to the Torah. He just made the blessings, and we threw a few candies. My parents and brothers and in-laws came for breakfast afterwards. It was a week of partying. On Friday several relatives came to sleep over in Kiryat Ganim and we all ate together in the yeshiva's dining room.

On Friday night, when Shimmy got undressed, I discovered a serious problem: he had split the pants of his Bar Mitzvah suit! I showed the pants to my mother-in-law. I felt like laughing and crying. It was the Sabbath — and of course I could not sew the seam then. What would he wear when he was called to the Torah the next morning?!

My mother-in-law came to the rescue — she borrowed an entire package of safety pins and pinned the whole ripped back seam.

The next morning I helped Shimmy carefully get into his pinned pants. He was worried about getting pricked by the pins and was reluctant to put them on. I promised him that once prayers were over, he could change — I had a hard time not giggling over my Bar Mitzvah boy's pants!

Once in *shul*, it seemed to me that all of Kiryat Ganim had come for Shimmy's Bar Mitzvah. Most had come because they cared for Shimmy. As I sat there my stomach was churning and I was filled with anxiety: How would Shimmy do in his public reading of the *Haftarah*? Let it just be over! I thought.

Chaya and I began distributing to the women and girls the candies we had brought to *shul*. The women enjoy having an "active" role: throwing candies into the men's section! Some of the young boys are happy for an excuse to pelt their friends, and the little children love picking up the candies that fall.

As soon as Shimmy was called up to read the *Haftarah*, a hush descended upon the *shul*. As I held my breath he recited the blessings and began to chant the traditional melody in a clear, quick tempo. It was beautiful: no mistakes, no mispronunciations. Shimmy had read the *Haftarah* perfectly.

Immediately upon finishing, he took off his hat and put a *tallis* over his head. Covered by the prayer shawl, he was ready for the onslaught of candies.

I wiped my eyes with a tissue and joyously reciprocated the *Mazal tov* wishes and kisses from my mother, mother-in-law, sisters, Chaya and all the women, many of whom were wiping their eyes, too. Shimmy had touched many hearts. We were all so proud of him.

Without any prompting, he took off the *tallis*, and instead of returning to his seat, he left the men's section and came into the women's section to give me a hug and a kiss. No one had even suggested this to Shimmy. He has a special sensitivity to other's feelings, and just knew I wanted to give him a great big hug at that moment.

I was full of love for my "little man."

Epilogue

IT TOOK ME over five years to write this book. During summer vacation and Jewish holidays, when the children were all at home, I did not even attempt to sit down and write. While working on a fundraising affair for Limudei Hashem, for the yeshiva in Kiryat Ganim, or for the local *cheder*, I would be too busy to find a quiet hour to write. And even during "uneventful" periods, managing a family of seven young children did not leave me much free time. But besides all the objective reasons that made the writing difficult, there was also a subjective one.

There have been periods when Shimmy suddenly seemed to have a total slump or cessation of developmental growth. There were times, especially with the onset of adolescence, when he became very angry and unhappy, yelling for no apparent reason and unwilling to listen to anyone.

When things looked bleak I would think, Who am I to write a book? What can I tell a mother with a stubborn child, with a child who doesn't seem to be progressing? I have no answers. I do not even know what the future holds for my own son and for my family.

One day when Shimmy was fourteen, he came home from school furious. A schoolmate had teased him, Shimmy had begun screaming in class, and the Rebbe had punished him by taking off merit points. Distraught and angry, Shimmy threatened never to return to school. He did not want anyone to talk to him or look at him.

Yona responded with, "Okay, we won't talk to you."

Shimmy was burning. "I told you not to talk!"

Yona was not to be stopped. "Okay, we won't talk!!"

"Be quiet!"

"I am being quiet."

Shimmy became so worked up that I had to run and rescue Yona from a beating. It took an hour for Shimmy to calm down — but once he had calmed down, he apologized to me and to each of his siblings whom he had upset. During the terrible hour of his fury all kinds of thoughts went through my head: His behavior is so irrational — maybe he'll never be able to interact with people normally; maybe he needs much more professional help. I was very worried. Yehoshua was far away in America — to whom could I turn for help with this "violent" Shimmy?

The next day, when baby Shlomo was taking his morning nap, I hesitated to take out my notebook and write as I often did, for what kind of ending could this book have? Why write something that would not offer hope? It took me a few days, and a consultation with a staff member at Limudei Hashem, to sort out my feelings and thoughts. I took up my pen again when I came to some realizations.

Shimmy was an adolescent and was "acting out" as adolescents often do. Possibly he was louder than some other teenagers, but not necessarily. Because he was overweight he could look somehow threatening when angry. Yet, all things considered, Shimmy's behavior was not so out of the ordinary. Once I acknowledged that and ceased being unduly worried, I found I could deal with him more effectively. I worked at keeping my own temper under control, and that helped too.

During the period of one of Shimmy's adolescent slumps (that is how I would refer to them) a neighbor called me up. She had no idea that I was in a bit of a slump myself over Shimmy. She just called, she explained, because she wanted to share with me her appreciation of Shimmy.

"Yesterday," she went on, "I was at the playground along with about a dozen other mothers and loads of children. We were all just sitting there and chatting while keeping an eye on our children. A taxi pulled up and let out a passenger, Rabbi Safran [an elderly resident of Kiryat Ganim]. He got out of the taxi and began putting all his many packages and purchases in order, while the driver unloaded several bags from the trunk and then drove away.

"Well," she continued, "as Rabbi Safran was struggling to assemble all his packages, suddenly your Shimmy appeared. He took three bags in one hand, and two in the other, and proceeded to walk Rabbi Safran all the way home.

"I must tell you, Rivka, I felt so embarrassed that I had not jumped up to help. It was so beautiful to see that Shimmy, only a child, had without any hesitation run to assist an older person."

It was good to hear from someone else that my child was appreciated. It made me realize I too should make it a point to recognize the good in Shimmy — and, in fact, in everyone.

I also devoted several hours to thinking about why I was writing this book. I have read many books on learning disabilities and handicaps, and the books that were most helpful to me were those dealing with real children and their stories. Theories and explanations afforded some ideas for me, yet when I read about other real families or specific cases, I gained more insights in dealing with my own situation. I also came to the conclusion that since some of my problems were not uncommon, it must mean that things were not only my fault! Like all mothers, I cannot help but feel responsible for my children's behavior. Yet, the reality is that parents cannot and should not be held responsible for all of their children's actions or problems. We should be open to accepting guidance when we have a problem, and we need to make an effort to improve things. But indulging in guilt feelings is a waste of energy.

Hopefully, some professionals will also read this and gain insight into the dilemmas of the parents of handicapped children. Labeling a child may give some direction to his teachers, but overall, labeling is simply wrong. Diagnoses can change, and often initial labels are incorrect and misguide those trying to work with the child. Moreover, a label, in its finality, stigmatizes the child and disheartens the parents. It may cause parents, children and professionals to resign themselves to the child's limitations. Rather, everyone should be encouraged to try and overcome or compensate for difficulties. A label makes this very difficult.

A child who is totally blind may never see with his eyes, but he does not have to be limited in what he can experience in the world through his other senses. This can apply to a child with visual perceptual difficulties as well. He may learn to perceive and understand what is before him through cues from his non-visual senses.

We parents have to try to give all our children the best we can. We must acknowledge this and accept the responsibility of enlisting for them the maximum of help. We have to accept that others may have more expertise than we do, but though we need the professionals, it is wiser not to step out of the picture entirely. As parents our input and instinct are invaluable. It is we who care the most. It is a difficult matter to balance — we must rely on those who are trained to understand, to provide help for our children with disabilities, yet at the same time we need to be part of the team in making the best decisions for them.

Faith and prayer are important in facing all of life's situations, and certainly so in situations like these. To acknowledge God's hand in our lives, His wisdom and His guiding love, makes it easier to bear. Prayer and our dependence on His help and intervention are invaluable.

A mother once asked me, "Don't you feel worthless when someone rejects your son?" This made me recall the very painful experience Yehoshua and I endured when a Jerusalem *cheder* refused to accept Yona. We had been hurt by the principal's insensitivity.

"Your son won't fit in here," he told us. "The other boys will make fun of him. Our school is on a very high level." At the time I had bitterly replied, "I'm surprised to hear that the educators of Jerusalem are so concerned with the status of their schools. And who will be concerned with Jewish children seeking a Jewish education?"

I remembered that and answered the mother: "No, I don't feel worthless. Perhaps such words of rejection are meant to put me or my son down, but, thank God, I know that none of us is worthless. All our children are part of *Klal Yisrael* — the Congregation of Israel!"

When I think of that principal now, I am still angry. Why should he have anticipated that the children would make fun of Yona? Whose attitude would they have been reflecting, I wonder.

I have written this book to remind all educators that their responsibility is not only to impart knowledge, but to teach *middos* — good traits and qualities. They are meant to exemplify the behavior we want our children to assume.

Once a mother of a five-year-old girl approached me. She was finding it hard to accept the results of her daughter's latest IQ test. Her own family — all her brothers and sisters — were very intelligent and highly educated. When a psychologist had labeled her child "retarded" and declared that she should put her into a special school for the retarded, the mother had felt physically sick.

The mother had then consulted another specialist who recommended a different diagnostic kindergarten where the children were not given definite labels. I told her that I had gone through a similar experience, and that thank God, Shimmy had ultimately found the place that was best for him.

"I have been especially blessed with a useful characteristic," I told her. "When something awful happens, I just forget the pain and relegate it to a forgotten memory. Try and forget the unpleasant encounter with the psychologist, and enjoy your daughter's obvious improvement."

I related this incident to Chana, another mother who was discussing with me her experience in finding a special school for her four-year-old. We were sitting on a bench in the Kiryat Ganim playground, and I was enjoying watching Chana's chubby daughter Leah climb the ladder of the slide with my Shlomo.

"When Leah was born," her mother told me, "she was very weak and floppy. In fact, she could not even pick up her head until she was a year old. It took us several months until we were able to find the right doctor who could help. At the point that Leah could lift her head, this caring doctor insisted we take a picture of her.

"He said, 'I want you to remember Leah at this stage, so that when she's five and not running fast enough you will remember and be able to appreciate how far she's progressed.'"

Chana concluded, "It's best to try and forget the pain and all the bad feelings. Yet it's important to remember to appreciate each small step of improvement."

I hope that as the general public becomes more informed and aware of what learning disabilities are, people will also become more accepting of this problem. It is essential to realize that although some children may have specific difficulties, they are still children — children with difficulties — and not difficult or disabled children.

Each parent and educator hopefully will become aware of a child who is having a hard time. Knowledge gives us the ability to be aware and discerning. If I were to list the steps needed to help a child with delays, the first step would be the parents' admitting and acknowledging to themselves that something is not perfectly right with their child, that something is wrong.

The next steps are technical, and they can vary in order. This is the procedure I would suggest for a concerned parent who sees a problem:

1- Have a competent pediatrician give your child a complete physical examination. The doctor has general guidelines for determining the appropriateness of your child's physical, mental and emotional growth.

2- Your child's vision and visual perception, and his hearing, should be checked by proper professionals. Short attention span can actually be the result of poor vision or a hearing impairment. These problems need specific corrective measures.

3- If no physical handicap is apparent and a child seems to have a delay or high distractibility, a neurologist and a psychologist are the next professionals to be consulted.

4- A speech and language therapist, as well as an occupational therapist can, with testing, pinpoint specific areas of weakness and strength.

The findings of the above professionals, together with the observations and input of caring parents, can help solve the mystery of why a child is having a difficult time in school or among his peers — or why the child is giving his parents trouble.

At that point, and even before the mystery is thought to be solved, the major emphasis should be on finding a suitable educational facility. Children need to be in a structured environment (nursery, kindergarten, school). Auxiliary help can be crucial in furthering a child's development, but first, a child needs to be in the right class.

At this time I know that testing is done, at no expense to the parent, in the United States, Canada and Israel. Some free therapy can also be found. The disadvantage of going through the government systems for testing, however, is that there is often a wait of several months involved. When parents finally come to the stage of accepting the fact that their child needs help, it is particularly frustrating to then be delayed.

Going to private doctors can be very expensive! If one has to choose how to allocate a limited amount of money I would recommend maximizing therapy. However, if a parent feels that a diagnosis is way off and the report may damage his child's potential for appropriate placement, it is vital to seek a skilled sympathetic professional.

Certainly not all parents are in a position to start their own program or class. There are so many circumstancial factors necessary for it to work out. For me it was especially important because I could not personally work with Shimmy, but some parents are excellent in advancing their children on their own.

Like our children, we must maximize our own potential. We need to help them grow, and yet we must also accept them with their limitations, recognizing that all our children are a gift from God.

Glossary

The following glossary provides a partial explanation of some of the Hebrew and Yiddish (Y.) words and phrases used in this book. The spellings and explanations reflect the way the specific word is used herein. Often, there are alternate spellings and meanings for the words.

ABBA: father.

ADON OLAM: "Master of the Universe," the opening words of the song of praise at the close of the Sabbath morning prayer service.

ALEF: the first letter of the Hebrew alphabet.

BA'AL KOREH: one who reads aloud from the Torah for the congregation.

BEIS: the second letter of the Hebrew alphabet.

BEIS HA-MIDRASH: the study hall of a yeshiva.

BEIS HA-MIKDASH: the Holy Temple.

BUBBIE: (Y.) grandmother.

CHEDER: (Y.) a religious primary school for boys.

CHUMASH: [one of] the Five Books of Moses.

HAMENTASHEN: (Y.) jelly-filled triangular cookies traditionally baked for Purim.

IMMA: mother.

KIPPAH: a skullcap.

KLAL YISRAEL: the Jewish nation.

LASHON HA-RA: slander; malicious gossip.

MAZAL TOV: "Congratulations!"

MECHITZAH: a partition separating the men from the women in a synagogue or at a religious affair.

MEGILLAH: a scroll; the Scroll of Esther.

MIDDOS: good attributes.

MINYAN: a minimum of ten adult male Jews, the quorum for congregational prayer.

MITZVOS: the 613 Torah commandments.

MORAH: (f.) teacher.

NACHES: (Y.) pleasure and satisfaction.

OLIM: lit., "ascenders"; immigrants to Israel.

PARASHAS HA-SHAVUA: the weekly Torah portion.

PTACH: "Open!"

PEYOS: sidelocks.

SABA: grandfather.

SAVTA: grandmother.

SEUDAH: a festive meal.

SHALACH MANOS: (Y., colloq.) gift packages of food traditionally sent on Purim.

SHUL: (Y.) a synagogue.

SIDDUR: a prayer book.

SIMCHAH: a joyous occasion.

TALLIS: a prayer shawl.

TORAH SHE-B'AL PEH: the Oral Law.

TZORA'AS: a skin disease of Biblical times.

YESHIVA: an academy of Torah study.

YISHAR KO'ACH: (colloq.) "Well done!"

ZAIDIE: (Y.) grandfather.

Index